Heart of Healing, Heart of Light

Other titles by Flora Slosson Wuellner:

Prayer, Stress, and Our Inner Wounds

Prayer and Our Bodies

Prayer, Fear, and Our Powers:
Finding Our Healing, Release,
and Growth in Christ

Heart of Healing, Heart of Light

Encountering God,
Who Shares and Heals Our Pain

Flora Slosson Wuellner

UPPER
ROOM BOOKS
NASHVILLE

Heart of Healing, Heart of Light

cover transparency: © William James Warren / Westlight
cover design: Leigh Ann Dans
First printing: November 1992 (5)
Printed in the USA
ISBN 0-8358-0666-9

This book is dedicated
to my sisters and brothers,
lovers of God,
who have shared many of these experiences,
and whose lives have given me light:
Lucy Chase and Jim Bob
Mary and George
Edith and Dean
Ingeborg and Edwin

Contents

INTRODUCTION

THE HEART OF GOD, with us from the beginning, is being shown to us again, in a powerful, significant, and healing way.

Our awareness of God's heart, as revealed to us through the heart of Jesus Christ, is an ancient awareness. It has been experienced for hundreds of years as the deep personal identity and love of God. But at this time in our history, it seems to be manifested anew in many fresh and surprising ways. Is God reaching out to us again in this special way? Is our consciousness touched again by God's passionate, personal involvement with us?

This love, this offered healing, is with us always, of course. We need never plead with God to love us, to "have mercy on us," or to shine on us. God is love, and it is the nature of God the Beloved to be and do these things. That face which we seek already looks on us with infinite tenderness, drawing us closer with an eternal attraction.

In the first chapter of this book, I tell the story of a recent personal experience of the heart of Christ, which has changed many things for me. For me, it was more than a symbol or metaphor. It was a powerful, actual, healing presence.

Over the succeeding months, the meaning of this inner vision has continued to unfold, sometimes through inner spontaneous pictures and prayers, sometimes through the shared experiences of others.

Why do we not always experience the reality of this presence? Why do we not always feel the closeness and the power of that heart which holds us?

Sometimes I picture a little house in a meadow, surrounded by the warmth of the sun, the tall green trees, fresh air. But the windows of our house are tightly closed, the shades pulled down, the door locked. Inside our little house we sit in the darkness, striking matches for a few moments of light. We sit longing for light, pleading for light, wondering what we have done that the light has been taken away from us. We do not know, or we have forgotten, or we cannot believe that we are already surrounded by that light, the air, the green growing things. The very thing we long for, pray for, at this moment embraces us.

From the first book to the last, the scriptures tell us that God longs infinitely more than we do for our full awareness of that divine love that holds us. God hungers and thirsts and seeks for our awareness, our response, our healing and delight. And we are told that even though we may only be aware of darkness, God's love is there in the darkness with us, there next to us in our little locked houses, sharing our pain, holding us closely.

This book explores the meaning of the heart of God sharing our pain, offering us the light.

It explores the problems and blocks we experience as we seek to trust God's love and respond to it. It is a practical book that works with our unhealed wounds, our abused ability to trust, the infected anger that is not yet able to cleanse, the fatigue and draining we experience as we try to give and to love, and that strange feeling of God's absence that sometimes overcomes us.

It is a book of shared thoughts and personal experiences of the immediacy and power of God's heart, brought to us so fully through the living Jesus Christ.

Each chapter contains biblically based prayers and meditations, offered to help us hear what God is saying, to begin the inner healing, to open our hearts more widely to God, to explore our fears, to rebuild our trust, to explore and cleanse our anger, to renew our strength, to affirm our borders, to share more deeply God's pain and God's joy.

As you enter these meditations, either individually or with a group, never push yourself or allow anyone else to push you. The only authority is God's spirit within your heart. Trust your own timing, your own special way of responding. Never imitate another's response or try to contrive an "appropriate" response and experience.

The awareness of God's presence and guidance comes to us in many different ways: sometimes through inner picturing, sometimes through a word or phrase that rises spontaneously, sometimes through an emotional feeling, sometimes through an intuitive sensing, sometimes through a message from your body. If nothing special rises during prayer, it is enough just to claim God's presence (even if you cannot feel it), to rest, and to breathe gently, letting each breath remind you of God's breath of life breathed into you. Observe your bodily feelings at such times. Bodily awareness is just as powerful as is inner envisioning, since our bodies are given to us as our spiritual companions. Not everyone is able to respond to guided meditations with inner pictures, and we should release ourselves and others to alternative ways of deep prayer.

As you pray, sit or lie down in whatever position is most relaxed and comfortable. Or, walk around if that feels more natural. Listen to music, light a candle if you need a focusing center, or hold some picture or object in your hand that draws your attention to God. Feel free to use your five senses: touch, sight, hearing, taste, smell. Our senses are given to us as spiritual companions to help us become more aware of God. However, it is important to know that not everyone responds to these outer aids. Some people prefer to go quickly and deeply into an interior silence, beyond sensory aids, beyond inner words and pictures. Neither way is more holy than the other. A lot depends on your type of temperament and your particular need at the moment. You may well find yourself shifting back and forth between words and inner pictures or between words and inner stillness without words and pictures. It is the same with any relationship. Sometimes we want to talk and share feelings and experiences together; sometimes we just want to sit quietly in each other's presence.

If any of these suggested meditations do not feel right for you, claim your freedom to withdraw from the meditation. Change any of the metaphors or symbols. Or, move into some other form of prayer which is right for you at this time. Each relationship with God is unique. Each way of growing and opening is somewhat different from every other way. All we can do for one another is to share our own experiences with God, suggest aids and alternatives, but never to push or manipulate, or to compel imitation.

This book is based on the faith in the living Jesus Christ as a real presence among us; who not only lived in the flesh two thousand years ago, but who is still with us—an actuality, with even greater power to bless, guide, and heal us. This book is written in that name and under that guidance.

However, I am aware that there may be those reading this book who have been wounded in the name of Jesus, who were taught that Jesus would punish or compel them. It is a tragedy that the one who came to heal and release us has so often been portrayed as one who hurts and imprisons! If you were thus hurt, if you find it hard to trust Jesus, ask the Holy Spirit to heal that deep wound and to show you the *real* Jesus who fulfills and does not destroy. While that healing is in process, ask that God's healing light may come to you through some way or symbol that you *are* able to trust at this time.

As you read this book, as you enter into its suggested meditations, you may become aware of pain and problems as yet unexplored within you, which may take you by surprise. Or, you may rediscover old pain that you thought was in the past, but which instead is found to be still hurtfully present. Do not hesitate to seek God's healing touch through physicians, therapists, counselors, sharing groups, as well as through prayer. These prayers and meditations are not meant to be substitutes for any necessary professional help, but rather to enhance and enrich it.

Seek loving communities of faith: men and women also seeking to experience God's love more fully, and whose prayers and presence will help you.

As your opening, your healing, your growing continues to unfold, know that God, through the living Jesus, not only walks with you but has already gone ahead to prepare the next place for you.

Chapter One

THE HEALING POWER OF GOD'S HEART

IN APRIL 1990, a powerful inner vision came to me as I led a group in healing prayer.

Unexpectedly, spontaneously, I inwardly saw the living Jesus Christ, the Healer, standing in the dark prison of some indescribable human pain.

He stood there quietly, pressed on all sides by icy, dark stone. He was so imprisoned by the walls of stone, he could not move. The light from his body shone only for a few inches in the cold, engulfing darkness. I sensed the thick stone extended for miles above him, below him, on all sides. He was not struggling; he stood very still.

Where was this place? What was this cold, endless despair that closed around him? In whose pain had he entered so deeply? I heard nothing, but I sensed it was the pain of the whole human race.

I watched him, not knowing what to do, how to pray. Suddenly, radically, the whole inner picture changed. The living Jesus threw open his arms in a wide, embracing gesture. (Later, I realized this was also the cruciform gesture.) The heavy darkness collapsed in on itself and took the shape of a hurt, bleeding bird. The bird fled like a swift dart directly *into* Jesus' heart, into the core of his body. He folded sheltering hands over his heart, as if cradling the bird who had entered his heart.

As I watched, I realized that though it was a miracle that the living Jesus had entered our human darkness, it was even more a miracle that he was able to take that full pain into his own heart. This was deeper, more radical.

As best I could, I shared with the group what I had seen. But I was almost dazed with the surprise of it. I had never seen a picture of such a scene, nor had I ever read any such description. In the days and weeks that followed, I became aware that something had changed deeply in my ministry and in my relationship with God. My understanding of the meaning of Jesus with us had moved to a much deeper level. My way of praying, both for others and for myself, experienced an empowering change.

Something new began to happen in my counseling. People began to share appalling experiences of crisis, trauma, suffering far beyond anything I had ever heard before. A child psychologist told me horrifying details of a true case of ritual child abuse. A short time later, three survivors of such abuse, living in different parts of the country with no knowledge of each other, told me their own stories. On other cases, I heard of family cruelty almost past belief, and the resulting despair and destruction. Sometimes the sensing of dark pain was like a powerful and almost uncontrollable presence in the room.

But now I was aware of another, far more powerful presence: the Healer, the living Jesus, in that usually unseen but transforming body of light. I became aware at these times that not only was the Healer of light present with us but he was offering to take the full crushing impact of all that dark pain directly into his heart.

I sensed that I was there in the room to be present as a human being, listening, hearing, caring, loving. But I was also there to help *send* all those shattering, unbearable stories into the Healer's body and heart. I sensed I was told that this is what the living Savior is here for, to take the uncontrollable suffering, to receive it, internalize it, heal and transform it with God's own fire of love.

I was *not* there to carry the full suffering impact in my own body and heart. If I tried to do that, I would soon burn out, break into pieces, or harden into a rock. I could feel the actual movement of the tragic energies, there in the room, moving like a swift, dark, weeping current into the Healer's heart. This was unlike anything I had ever experienced before.

This inner vision has had tremendous implications, not only for these extreme cases of tragedy, but also for the more ordinary events of counseling, and for the everyday stresses of life.

To a lesser extent I had been aware for many years that any Christian, whether pastor or layperson, is in trouble if he or she tries to be the Source, the Vine, instead of the branch.

> Abide in me, and I in you. As the branch cannot bear fruit by itself unless it abides in the vine, neither can you unless you abide in me. I am the vine, you are the branches.
>
> —John 15:4-5

We are in trouble if we try to be the ultimate fountain of love for all comers. To change the metaphor, any shepherd of sheep who forgets that he or she also needs shepherding and nurture is in great danger of becoming heartbroken at the one extreme, or bitterly manipulative at the other.

The vine and branch metaphor changed my life and ministry many years ago. But the vision of the heart of God through the living Jesus is even more immediate, radical, and powerful.

I wonder if we have barely begun to realize, barely begun to scratch the surface of what the risen, living Jesus offers to do and is able to do for us, whether in our extremest suffering or in our daily work and relationships. I believe the new surfacing of the awareness of the heart of God and our own deep hearts in this decade is a way by which God is reaching out to our core selves at this time.

It is not really new, of course. It is an ancient way of understanding God and relating to God. The heart of God, the heart of Jesus, is found in many early prayers and writings. But we are reminded anew and afresh of this fiery center of passionate love and transformation.

When we are reminded, it seems to come to us with instinctive, almost bodily recognition as of a central reality within us.

I remember poignantly a time when my own bodily heart became a symbol for my anxieties about my own identity. It was 1939, just before the outbreak of the Second World War. Our whole family was in Europe for my father's study leave. I can remember the frightening blackouts and air raid drills in the great cities. I can still smell the rubber gas masks we all carried with us. Sandbags were piled in the streets in preparation for the bombings to come. Barbed wire was already stretched across future battlefields. Periodically, we would hear the voice of Hitler, screaming his way through a radio speech. All over Europe there were fleeing refugees, separated families, lost children. I think my parents had no idea how much I, as a child, was absorbing of this evil miasma spreading over our world. Actually, I was not clearly aware that I *was* frightened. But after several months in this atmosphere, I began, all of a sudden, to worry about my heart. I would lie in bed, wondering what kept it going. Lying awake, I would concentrate on its rhythm, trying to keep it beating by will power. If it skipped a beat (and of course it sometimes did under all that tension), I would panic. One night, I woke my older sister, there in the bed with me, sobbing and telling her that my heart had stopped altogether! First she reasoned with me that if it had really stopped, I would not be alive enough to talk at all. That scared me even more! She tried firmness, but by now I was out of control. Finally, with kindly strength, she took my hand in her own hand, and placed my palm on the center of my chest, keeping her hand warmly on top of mine.

"There," she said comfortingly. "I can feel your heart just fine. And now *you* can feel it, too, through both our hands." And as the warmth of our joined hands spread deeply into my heart area, I did begin to feel, at last, the strong, rhythmic beating. Comforted, I slept.

She and I laugh over this story now. It is obvious to me now, of course, that this intense focusing on my heart was rooted in my threatened identity and that of our family. Even though my family was a loving and secure one, how did I know my family would survive? The heart became for me the symbol of all that made life precious.

I had many similar fears during the early years of the war even after our return to the USA, fears centered on various symbols of deep identity and the core of life. I remember clearly the days when the real healing of these fears began. A family friend had been drafted into the army. The day he was to be sent overseas, we all got up at dawn to tell him good-bye, not knowing if we would ever see him again. After he left for the train station, I stood by my window, watching the dawn stars shining on the snow. Suddenly, I remembered some words I had read in the Bible,

It is the God who said
"Let light shine out of darkness,"
who has shone in our hearts
to give the light of the knowledge of the
glory of God
in the face of Jesus Christ.
—2 Corinthians 4:6

As I watched the morning stars and thought about these words, I felt a warmth begin to grow within my heart and spread throughout my whole body. I knew that if God indeed shone through the face of Jesus Christ into our hearts, if God were really like that, then all of us—myself, my family, my whole world—were in safe hands, no matter what happened outwardly. From that time, many fears began to heal for me.

The Bible speaks hundreds of times about our hearts as the spiritual center from which we love, respond to love, make choices, become aware. This is not surprising. The deep, pulsing rhythm of our mother's heartbeat was probably our first sensory experience, even before our own small heart began to respond with its own rhythm. That central rhythmic beat nurtures and enlivens us. Newborn babies love to sleep with their heads near the heartbeat of the father or mother. We love to dance to its beat. We find it in ethnic music for example, and in the sound of the waves on the shore. It is the pulse of life itself, slowing, speeding, according to the needs of our bodies and the power of our emotions.

If the heart is the ancient symbol for human identity and human vitality, it is also a powerful symbol for the fiery love of God.

The famous astronomer Sir James Jeans once wrote that the more he studied the mystery, complexity, and intelligence of the universe, the more he was convinced that the universe is not a great machine but a great thought. I believe we can go further and say that at the core mystery of the universe is not only a great thought but a supreme *heart*! This heart is not only the source and renewing spring of the universe, sustaining each particle of creation, but it also exists centrally within each particle, object, person, loving each part as if it were the whole.

Focusing on the heart of God draws us not only to the power and the intelligence, but even more to the personal involvement of God with us. It makes an almost immeasurable difference in our lives if the ultimate mystery has become personal for us. If we think of God and relate to God as impersonal, mechanical power our relationship to ourselves, to others, to the world around us is affected. Subtly, a deep current in impersonality, even de-personalization, can begin to flow through all that we are and do.

The heart relationship with God celebrates our full humanity. We are intended to grow *more* human, not less, as our love for God grows. This spirituality, which I call incarnational spirituality, does not make us remote, desireless, detached. When we respond to

God's heart from our own deep hearts, we bring the fullness of all our humanity into that relationship, our needs, longings, anger, grieving, joy, bewilderment, and we bond them to God.

Jesus had a warm, human personality. He was not ashamed to laugh, to cry, to show love and anger. When he challenges us to "be perfect" (Matt. 5:48), I do not believe he meant us to become inhumanly infallible, never making a human mistake. Rather, he was inviting us to experience wholeness, through the warmth of God's heart, learning to live in trust from that supreme and tender center.

Constantly I meet people who have been wounded by teachings that try to fence in the released life of Jesus. I have seen tragedies from teachings which build walls of judgment and condemnation, diagnosing, prescribing, punishing. Jesus rebelled against that kind of religion!

The heart of Jesus, as revealed in scripture and encountered in our personal lives, *is* a direct core experience of God's intimate heart. How can we begin to understand and describe the mystery of the relationship between the living Jesus and the eternal God? One way may be to think of God's love as a great circle of light surrounding us. But the circle of light does not just hold us. It also flows directly toward us, through the person of Jesus, making contact with our own hearts.

One spiritual leader put it this way: God's love is like the sunshine that radiates and animates the whole earth. The living personality of Jesus is like a magnifying lens, focusing the sun's rays so intensely that fire begins when the lens is held over dry leaves. A Christian is not one whom God loves more than others. Rather, a Christian is one who has gone under the empowering, focusing lens of Jesus' personality. Then fire begins in our hearts, the fire that does not destroy but which is a radiant warmth that enlivens us and all who come near us. This is what Jesus meant when he said, "I came to cast fire upon the earth; and would that it were already kindled!" (Luke 12:49). And this is what the great Saint Vincent de Paul of the seventeenth century meant when he reportedly said: "We are chosen by God to do what the Son of God did, Who came to bring fire to the earth, to inflame it with His Love!"

Perhaps another way to describe the experience of God through Jesus is to picture a child, waking, playing, eating, living all day surrounded by the presence and love of the family. But at some point during the day, the mother or father picks up and hugs the child, spends a special, personal hour with the child. This is the general love now experienced in an intense, direct, personal way.

I have noticed a creeping, infectious coldness and wilting in churches and in individual Christians who have lost that awareness of the personal, passionate, real presence of the living Jesus. So often we hold Jesus at arm's length, seeing him only as an admirable moral leader of two thousand years ago whom we are supposed to imitate. When this happens, our religion becomes boring and ineffective. It becomes savorless, like a lukewarm marriage in which the spouses seldom meet each other face to face, but try to keep the relationship alive through reading old love letters.

I remember a young pastor who talked with me. During the conversation, he became startlingly aware that the Jesus he had thought of, preached, and written about as an historical figure, a theological proposition, was actually alive and there in the room with him! He wept with joy and relief. *This*, and none other, is the fiery central core of our faith. Without it, we lose the transforming power. We may be moral, we may be righteous, we may have fine ideals and beautiful thoughts. But without this living presence, we Christians have lost our wind, fire, salt, and yeast.

The heart of God that we see through Jesus beats for us intensely and personally. It may be that you find this central focus on God's heart, Jesus' heart, as troubling or even frightening. For example, if you have had heart disease, or experienced organic pain and dysfunction in your heart, it may be a real problem to think of the heart, even God's heart, as a healthy power.

I found a helpful reference in that excellent book, *Kything: The Art of Spiritual Presence,* in which a study by the National Institute of Mental Health (NIMH) talks about the "conversation between the brain and the heart." The "heart" is referred to as the physical heart as well as the "subtle or spiritual heart." Joseph Chilton Pearce, who summarized the study, said: "Our physical pumping heart is the translating mechanism for consciousness, and the subtle heart is the generative force itself."[1]

This means we all have a deep, underlying heart center, far more powerful and resilient than our bodily heart, a center which does not experience pain, weakness, or disease. It is our inner spring, our center light always renewed which is our spiritual heart. It affects our whole body, nurturing, connecting, empowering, *including* our bodily hearts. And when it is time to leave our body in the transition of death, that radiant center, sustained by God, renews its power in our body of light, our immortal body.

Nevertheless, if the word *heart* in these meditations still troubles you, it is enough to think of, or to picture a

[1]Louis M. Savary & Patricia H. Berne, *Kything: The Art of Spiritual Presence* (New York: Paulist Press, 1988), p. 122.

radiant center of light within you connected with God's radiant light.

Some have shared with me another problem. "I don't want to unload all my darkness, pain, and anger on anyone, especially Jesus, whom I love. I'm afraid it will hurt him," one person told me, really worried. She had herself experienced much emotional pain, and dreaded the thought of sending that pain and darkness into someone else's heart. This is a real and loving concern which must be taken seriously.

But this is the mystery of the Savior:

> Surely, he has borne our griefs
> and carried our sorrows;
> . . . .
> . . . wounded for our transgressions.
> —Isaiah 53:4, 5

We hear these words sung with grave thunder every Christmas when *Messiah* is sung. This includes not only our sins, but also our wounds, our pain. All that hurts us is already shared and carried by that heart. We are only asked to give the full impact of the pain with *consent*. This is the meaning of the limitless love that has come to be with us. If we still feel troubled, it may be helpful to think of another woman's experience. When I shared with her this problem, she said "I just *asked* Jesus if he was willing to receive my full load of pain directly into his heart, and he inwardly told me he was here for that reason and was willing and able to receive it all."

No matter what we do, no matter what we feel, no matter the full crushing impact of pain we give to God, that heart of God through Jesus will not be shattered or destroyed or hardened. The fire of God's love is fed by its own fire, forever.

Meditation:

> And he (Jesus) came down with them and stood on a level place, with a great multitude of...people...And all the crowd sought to touch him, for power came forth from him and healed them all.
>
> —Luke 6:17-19

Do you feel you are carrying heaviness, pain, emptiness that you cannot even explore or express at this moment? Or do you just need to feel God's presence and nurture at this moment? Ask yourself if you are ready to reach out, to respond to that presence, which embraces and surrounds you, even if you cannot feel it.

If you feel ready, inwardly picture the living Jesus with you, perhaps kneeling, sitting, or standing in front of you or near you. It does not matter if you cannot picture his face. If inner picturing is difficult for you, just inwardly speak to that presence, or just think of Jesus' presence, even if you feel nothing.

If you feel you cannot yet trust Jesus because of teachings about him that have wounded or frightened you, ask for God's tenderness and light to flow to you in some other way. Sense or picture a loving presence with you in whatever way is best for you.

Relax your body, gently breathing. There is no hurry. Take all the time you need. Inwardly thank that radiant, healing presence with you. Sense or picture a light in the area of the heart of the Healer. Fix your inner eyes and attention on that light coming from the heart of the Healer.

Breathe it in. If you feel ready, sense or picture how it flows toward you, gently but warmly as sunlight.

You may wish to picture or think of a connection, like an umbilical cord, between that heart and your heart. Let the stream of light flow to your heart, through the cord, spreading to all parts of your body.

Lay your crossed palms on your own heart area, at the center of your chest, until you begin to feel the warmth of your hands. Hold them there without pressure, gently, inwardly praying: "The living love of Jesus Christ now fills me." Sense how the warm light of the living Jesus fills, calms, and heals your heart.

Rest in this presence, breathing quietly, thinking of your breath flowing through your heart, keeping your palms on your heart area as long as you need to. Fall asleep if you feel like it. It is beautiful to go into sleep through prayer. God continues to hold us, to speak to our deep selves, to heal us when we sleep.

Do not force or contrive any special feeling, but if any special feeling surfaces, or any hurtful problem rises, let it flow through the cord of light from your heart into the heart of the Healer.

When you feel ready, begin to become aware again of your surroundings, your bed, the chair, the floor beneath you, the sounds you hear outside or in the room.

Gently massage your face and hands if that feels right. Then open your eyes and stretch, bringing your meditation to a close.

Chapter Two

Our Pain and God's Heart

BUT IS THERE a heart of healing light and love at the center of the universe? Isn't the evidence all against it?

In the news, we hear of mass murders. I have just read of a hideous case of the abuse of a little child. A little boy has just been kidnapped. I know of a young woman paralyzed for life, the victim of a random shooting on a freeway. We have just received appeals for help for countries in the grip of epidemic cholera.

Recently in a church workshop, a pastor shared with us that he had been present at the deaths of dozens of men, women, and children killed by AIDS. He was devastated and exhausted. "Does God break our heart?" he asked. "How can we say any more that God's arms are holding us?"

Most of us, if we are honest, have had times of doubt and anguish, when we wonder if God is in control at all. Does God really love us, in the way love is usually understood?

We have already known, of course, that human

beings have always suffered in wars, diseases, crimes. But when suffering breaks into our personal lives, perhaps for the first time we ask ourselves the great, grave questions: Is God really with us? Does God really care? Can God really help?

I am in a specialized ministry which focuses on the healing of our inner wounds. As I lead retreats and teach and counsel, I ask and hear about the hurts of people, emotional hurts of infancy and early childhood, communal hurts passed down through the generations, suffering internalized from others around us, signals and symptoms of pain deeper than memory.

Is it that God cannot stop our suffering? If so, then is God weak, powerless? Or is it that God will not stop our suffering? If so, then is God merciless, without pity? Which is worse, the "cannot" or the "will not"?

When I ask myself these questions, I have learned to look directly to Jesus' life and words, as shown in the stories about him in the Gospels. What is shown to us about our pain and God's heart? I see three clear lights:

> God does not send us our pain.
> God enters into our pain and shares it with us.
> God is able to bring deep healing and
>   transformation from within.

What do these insights mean? First, God does not send our pain. It is an ancient and evil heresy that God sends our tragedies. Jesus denied this teaching. Not once in the four Gospels does Jesus say to anyone who asked for healing and help, "No, I won't heal you. God has sent this suffering to you, and it is good for your soul that you suffer."

Sometimes the Gospels imply that the full healing

of suffering was blocked. This may not necessarily be due to individual lack of faith or resistance, but perhaps more due to rigid, confused, frightened mindsets of the community which can fill the spiritual atmosphere like a thick fog. There is still such fear of God among us, though Jesus never taught the fear of God. Sometimes this is due to early abuse in childhood by those who have power and authority over us. Sometimes it is due to teaching by church or family (based on misunderstanding of the deep heart of scripture) that God is wrathful, vengeful, watching us relentlessly for mistakes, quick to condemn and punish.

Even if we were fortunate enough not to be taught these things, it is hard to become healed and released from the subconscious impact of centuries. For thousands of years, up to fairly recent centuries, there is evidence that in many of the religious cultures of the world, human sacrifice (including child sacrifice) was considered the acceptable way to show devotion to and receive favors from the gods. Human blood had to be shed, either in devotion or in repentance; or, it was taught, the gods would punish the community. Apparently this was almost a worldwide misunderstanding of God, with very few exceptions. Only in the last three thousand or so years was this hideous religious practice challenged in some cultures by brave prophets. But would not the thousands of years of fear and human sacrifice have left its deep wounds upon the communal human spirit? I believe that in our communal subconscious we still carry those unhealed scars of fear of God.

If anyone teaches of a punishing, vindictive God who condemns and sends tragedy and disaster, we should cling boldly to the living presence of Jesus Christ who shows us the true heart of God.

But what about the cross? Did not Jesus accept the cross? Did he not call us to take up our cross? A cross is not an illness or disaster sent us against our will and consent. Jesus' cross, our cross, is our free choice to become compassionately involved in the pain of others and to become part of the healing community to heal and transform that suffering.

So many have been wounded and frightened by mercilessness practiced in the name of God and Jesus. It must be one of the deepest sorrows of God's heart that religions have used threat, repression, condemnation, and punishment all in the name of God. Also, many of the words we use to name God have become meaningless, or have become associated with pain and problems. *King, Lord, Shepherd*—words once full of rich significance—mean little or nothing in urban cultures in the twentieth century which know little or nothing of kings, lords, shepherds. If we have come from dysfunctional or abusive families, the name father or mother for God may arouse anger or fear in their wounding associations. Traditional metaphors for God are too often closely related to fear of God.

I have found that different names for God come to us with comfort and strength at different times of our lives, according to our needs, if we can become open and expectantly released. If metaphors and names for God help us and heal our fear, I believe we should use them boldly without apology, but at the same time remain sensitive to the fact that others may be wounded or frightened by the metaphor that helps us. Everyone should be explicitly released and encouraged in church services, prayer groups, or conversation to speak of God and to God in whatever way is most meaningful and healing to that person. For myself, though blessed with a loving father and mother, and though I knew many good shepherds when I was pastor in sheep-grazing country, the name I love best for God is simply "Beloved."

The second great light that Jesus reveals about human suffering, is that God enters into and shares our pain. This is one of the deep meanings of the cross. It was the ultimate sign, witness, that God's heart never stands apart, but enters the utmost extent of our pain with us and bears the full impact for us.

Jesus had a vision of the culmination and ultimate challenge of God's heart to all nations and communities, to enter and identify with the pain of the homeless, the hungry, the ill, the imprisoned. God's real presence has entered these helpless, powerless ones: "Truly, I say to you, as you did it to one of the least of these...you did it to me" (Matt. 25:40). God's own fiery holiness abides with these very ones who have been labeled and treated as outcast and unworthy.

In the story of the Good Samaritan, for example (Luke 10:29-37), it is not always realized that the probable reason that the "righteous" passed by the wounded man was that he was certainly bleeding, and might even have been dead, and therefore was contaminated, impure to touch. A purification ritual would have been required before any who touched him could enter into their religious duties.

But according to Jesus in that twenty-fifth chapter of Matthew, God's own body, God's own presence was in that wounded, bleeding man, just as God's real presence was also in that Samaritan (an unorthodox person from a suspect community!). One of the main points of this story is that God's love and presence cannot be boxed in by our categories of righteousness. God's real presence, we can be very sure, is exactly where it is darkest. Every pain inflicted, every injustice, every cruelty has been done to the body of God, the heart of God. In every abusive home where a child cries in fear and pain, the living Christ, God's presence, is there ....hurting, sharing. In the city streets at night where homeless people are shivering under newspapers on the pavement, the living Christ is there... hurting, sharing.

I have always been haunted by the verses in the old and poignant hymn "Where Cross the Crowded Ways of Life":

> In haunts of wretchedness and need,
> On shadowed thresholds dark with fears,
> From paths where hid the lures of greed,
> We catch the vision of your tears.
>
> From tender childhood's helplessness,
> From woman's grief, man's burdened toil,
> From famished souls, from sorrow's stress,
> Your heart has never known recoil.

To enter these places is our cross too. But we cannot enter that pain and darkness, we cannot go to those frontiers of cruel evil, unless we go with the heart of the Christ enfolded around us, carrying us, going ahead to prepare the way for us.

This is true not only of the loveless, frightened, hurting communities around us, but also the loveless, frightened, cold, weeping community *within* us. The living Christ is there also, sharing, suffering with, ministering to our inner pain and fear.

But *why* does God choose to enter and share the full impact of our pain? *Why* did Jesus to go the cross and take the thrust of the spear into his side through to his heart? Why is all this necessary? Why does not God simply put a stop to the hideous suffering in this world? Many of us must be asking this question almost with despair this week as we hear in the news of a four-year-old girl snatched from her neighborhood. The suffering of her parents, the suffering of the child herself is unbearable to imagine. Yes, we know that the living Jesus is with that little girl and her parents, sharing, carrying the pain. But why is such suffering permitted at all?

I believe that God's power refuses to use force over us. When God created this world and humanity, God intended we should be free lovers whose choices arise from free decision, not mechanical puppets with no alternatives. God has taken enormous risks to create such a world in which we are free to choose, free to make mistakes. But would any other way have had any significant meaning at all? God has entered into the costs of this risk. God does not stand apart, observing. While we make mistakes, learn, grow, struggle, refuse or consent to love, use or abuse our freedom, God's heart shares the full experience.

Even if this alone were all, it would be a mystery, a miracle, an endless solace and strength. But this is not all! There is more. There is the third light.

God, the Beloved, renouncing force, coming into our darkness, taking our darkness into that heart, has promised total transformation by working from within us. If we consent freely to God's touch, the radical healing will unfold, radiating within each cell of our bodies, each wound of our hearts.

Jesus spoke of the yeast, expanding within the bread, the seeds opening and pushing up through the dark earth, a baby being born from its small, dark enclosure. He used many metaphors of the transformation working from within, expanding from the inner center.

Healing changes will be manifest, some slowly, some swiftly, some fully, some partially. Even if our body has reached the point where death is the best healing, usually our pain will be relieved. If we have lost some organic part, other organs will be strengthened to compensate. If sight, hearing, movement are not restored (and sometimes they are), other ways of sensing and responding unfold.

As God's healing light expands and radiates within, we will learn new ways of loving and honoring our bodies, so that they can work with our spirits as beloved partners, fully and gladly. I have seen miracles of bodily transformation when we consent to God's radical healing light within us and learn how to respond and cooperate with it.

Even more, I have seen miracles of transformation in the emotional lives of those whose inner wounds are being healed, whose frightened memories are entered by Jesus, whose dark, hidden places are compassionately and powerfully lit by the Healer.

I have seen miracles of transformed human relationships when Christ the Healer is given a "free hand." Even after two thousand years we have barely begun to understand and experience what can be done, what is promised when we ask the heart of the living Jesus to enter and take form within our own hearts.

It is one of the miracles that we discover that our pain (though not sent by God) is not wasted. When our wound is healed and transformed, there comes about a deeper unfolding of the light. Our healed wound becomes itself a life-giver. I am thinking of those whose life-threatening diseases have inspired them to start groups of comfort, information, and support to others experiencing that disease. I am also thinking of those whose children have been kidnapped or have been killed by drunken drivers and who have started nationwide organizations of reform and support.

Mysterious words once came to me in a dream: "Out of the ashes rises the healer." I think it probable that every great advance of the human race into deeper creative love has risen out of someone's transformed wound. God did not send the suffering, but if the suffering comes, God will not waste it, but will help us become deeper lovers, more compassionate healers, because of it.

Meditation

> The Spirit of the Lord GOD is upon me,
> . . . .
> to bring good tidings to the afflicted,
>   ...to bind up the brokenhearted,
> to proclaim liberty to the captives,
>   and the opening of the prison
>   to those who are bound;
>   to comfort all who mourn;
>   to give them a garland instead of ashes,
> the oil of gladness instead of mourning,
>   a garment of splendor in place of
>   grieving tears,
> that they may be called oaks of
>   righteousness,
> . . . .
> They shall build up the ancient ruins,
>   they shall raise up the former devastations;
> they shall repair the wounded cities,
>   the devastations of many generations.
>   —Isaiah 61:1-4

Jesus quoted these powerful words when he came out of the desert filled and radiant with his ministry of total compassion and healing (see Luke 4:16-19). Let now these words be spoken to you, personally. Picture, sense, or claim the actual presence of the risen, living Jesus in the room with you, near you, with the central light burning and shining in his heart.

Relax your body, breathing gently. Remind yourself you are in a safe place with God, the Beloved. When ready, turn your thoughts to your wounds and hurts.

Are you brokenhearted? God's heart, the heart of Christ, there in the room with you, shares all you feel and offers to carry its full weight.

Do you feel unfree, captive, imprisoned in your life and spirit? The risen Christ, the mighty one, who comes in power without force, longs for your freedom and is able to free you.

Are you mourning, deeply sad, depressed? The Beloved grieves with you, weeps with you, sits with you in the dimness, and will send the Holy Spirit, the "Comforter."

Do you feel that your life is in ashes? If you bond with the living Jesus, you will rise from the ashes in undreamed beauty and healing power.

Have you been wounded from generations of a hurting family or some other wounded community? If you take this full pain into the Healer's heart, you will be released from the "devastations of many generations" and will release a powerful current of healing into that family history.

You may not yet be able fully to believe these promises, to trust this presence, or to feel this power. Do not try to contrive appropriate feelings. At this point, just simply hear what is being offered. The healing of truth, the ability to open to God's heart, often comes very slowly. Just rest quietly, breathing gently, while the promises from God's heart are given in your presence.

When you feel ready, become aware of your body, then of your surroundings. Stretch; gently rub your face and hands; and end your meditation.

Chapter Three

LEARNING TO TRUST GOD'S HEART

IT IS ONE THING to be told that God is limitless love. It is another thing to learn to trust that heart.

The healing of our wounded ability to trust begins with honesty about our hurt and our doubt. Some years ago I read a well-meaning religious article which advised Christians to give up all grumbling, all negative thinking. The article suggested that whenever a doubt, a negative thought, a grumble made itself felt, we should immediately quench it, turn away from it, and substitute a positive attitude.

As I read this advice, I felt a wave of rebellion. This did not show awareness of the human condition. It was not incarnational spirituality. It did not reach down to the roots of our real problems, our real hurts that Jesus came to heal rather than to cover up. We cannot be fully healed until we know we *are* hurting. I thought of the grim words of the prophet Jeremiah:

They have healed the wound
of my people lightly,
saying, "Peace, peace,"
when there is no peace.
—Jeremiah 6:14

We are told in the Gospel of Mark (10:46-52) that a blind beggar, Bartimaeus, sat by the roadside, persistently shouting at Jesus, calling to him for help. Many in the crowd tried to hush him, but Bartimaeus would not let himself be silenced. He knew he had a real need, an honest need, and he was going to speak up and make it known without apology. Jesus, who built much of his ministry on interruptions, turned at once and called Bartimaeus to come to him and tell him what he needed.

Within each of us there is a Bartimaeus, calling out for healing and help. Sometimes it calls through puzzling bodily symptoms, sometimes through symptoms of anxiety, irritability, grumbling, nagging. Most of our lives we have either ignored this inner Bartimaeus, silenced it, or gone to the other extreme of just giving into it without really listening to the deep need. Neither, of course, is respectful of the inner cry of pain and need.

A far more powerful and effective spiritual discipline would be to learn how to turn fully and respectfully to our inner negative feeling—just as Jesus turned fully to Bartimaeus—and ask it, "What are you trying to tell me? What is the deep need here that God wants me to know about?"

This honesty, this attentive listening to our inner cry is a great, healing step toward learning to trust God. We have so often been taught that God will be offended or impatient with our needs. But God already knows all about our inner wounds, doubts, and fears; and God wants *us* to know about them.

One of the Bible stories that helps me the most in learning to trust God, is found in the Gospel of John, the twentieth chapter. After the death of Jesus, and after the rumors about his resurrection began to circulate, the disciples met behind closed doors. To their amazement, Jesus came to them through the tightly shut doors, and spoke to them lovingly and challengingly, promising them the peace and power of the Holy Spirit. They were comforted, reassured, joyful. But eight days later, when they met a second time, the door was tightly shut *again!*

When Jesus again came to them through the closed doors, he did not rebuke or condemn them for their fear. He understood that they had been deeply traumatized by the events of the week: the betrayal by Judas whom they had trusted; the denial by Peter who had seemed so strong; the arrest, trial, and execution of Jesus; the hideous shame and shock of the crucifixion; the continuing persecution; the almost unbelievable resurrection. He undoubtedly understood that they hardly knew who or what to trust any more.

Likewise, God does not condemn *us* for our wounded ability to trust. You and I often tightly close our inner doors out of confusion, fear, and pain. God understands that our inner defenses, our emotional armor, our separating walls have grown in us for a reason. And this God of limitless mercy will not kick down our doors, tear off our masks and armor, or go away angry. This God, whom we see through Jesus, will continually come to us *through* our defensive doors, to be with us in power and comfort in our darkness.

I learned this in a strange way when I was fourteen. I was very close to my grandmother. When I was two years old she had come to live with us after she was widowed, so I could not remember a time when she was not there. She was a remarkable woman of great charm and intelligence: a teacher, writer, painter. She was a dear companion to me while I was growing up in our large and busy family. One of my earliest memories is taking long walks with her while she pointed out the amusing squirrels, leaping from branch to branch. In so many ways she helped me become aware of the beauty and curiosity of the world around us. Gentle, wise, close to God, she had a profound influence on me.

One night, just before dawn, I was wakened suddenly by banging doors, running footsteps. I went out sleepily into the hall, and saw a light in my grandmother's room and heard her groaning in pain. I heard my father telephoning the doctor, and then heard the words "heart attack." The house was in confusion, and I knew someone very dear to me was in pain and dying. Oddly enough I was not aware of fear or grief. I felt nothing at all, consciously. I turned back to my room, walked into my clothes closet, shut the door firmly behind me, and sat on the floor in the dark. I wasn't crying. I wasn't praying. I wasn't doing anything at all. I just sat there, silent, cold, and numb, expecting and feeling nothing.

Suddenly, I knew someone was there with me in the closet. The door was still shut; I didn't hear or see anything. But I knew someone was there in the dark with me, standing quietly in front of me. Then I felt strong, warm hands enfolding my cold hands. It felt as if the hands were holding my inner hands, rather than my outer, bodily hands. I felt pulled gently to my feet, and a sense of warmth filled my whole body. I opened the door and walked out of the closet. Somehow I knew, somehow I had been told (though I had heard no spoken words) that whether my grandmother lived or died, she was all right. She was safe. The same warm, powerful tenderness that surrounded me was also surrounding her.

She died early the next morning. As I looked at her face, I knew with certainty that she was indeed all right. She had stepped out of her body, but she was still with the One whose love had enfolded her always.

"God's presence does not stop where our skin begins," someone once said to me. We may not always be aware of God. We may not always be able to respond to the love and light, to the Heart that surrounds us. But that does not prevent that love from entering our darkness and sharing the pain of it with us.

Though that time I was able to open my door and walk out, I am not always so trusting. Repeatedly I have closed my inner doors. How much harder it would have been for me if I had experienced abuse of trust by those near me in my childhood. I meet so many men and women whose earliest memories have been of fear, violence, or cold detachment. If a child's parents, who represent ultimate power to a child, are abusive or emotionally absent, how much healing is needed before that child and the later adult can trust anyone or anything calling itself an ultimate power.

Again, I am reassured by that wonderful twentieth chapter in the Gospel of John. Even though the risen Christ had come to the disciples, Thomas had not been there that first time and did not believe his friends when they told him of their experience. When Jesus came the second time, he turned to Thomas and said,

"Put your finger here, and see my hands; and put out your hand, and place it in my side" (John 20:27). He did *not* say "Come here and embrace me at once." He encouraged Thomas to move slowly towards recognition and trust. First, "put your finger here." We can begin our trustfulness in small, tentative, exploring ways, with just one finger, metaphorically speaking. Then, "Put out your hand...." And as our trust deepens we become more bold, reaching back to God, touching God with our whole hand instead of just a finger. Then, as our certainty grows that God is here, God is trustworthy, we may be able to say at some point with Thomas: "My Lord, and my God" (John 20:28).

There is an ancient Christian tradition that Thomas, who at first doubted most, went the furthest of all the disciples, all the way to India to carry the good news of God's love!

There is far too much talk in many religious groups about the necessity of total surrender and trust as the first step of Christian growth. For some people this may be possible. For others, wounded from early years in their ability to trust, it is spiritual abuse to be ordered to take "leaps of faith" or to be told that they must immediately "let go and let God."

When I first learned to swim in deep water, I was ashamed that I was such a timid late bloomer. I knew how to swim, but deep water frightened me. If I could not touch the bottom of the pool with my toes, I panicked. Far too often, well meaning friends had pushed me into the water at the deep end saying cheerfully, "You must trust the water to hold you up!" Every time I would sink, bubbling, to the bottom! Finally, I found a merciful swimming pool which had a deep, curved hand hold all the way around the pool just below the edge, which I could easily grip with my fingers while in the water. Each day I went to the pool, entered at the shallow end, and, while holding tightly to the hand hold I would inch my way down to the deep end. I would wait until I felt relaxed, and then let go and swim a few feet toward the pool's center. I knew at any moment I could swim back to my safe hand hold. Within a week I had learned to swim in deep water, not only fearlessly but joyfully!

"I believe; help my unbelief!" cried out the loving, frightened father of a desperately sick child to Jesus (Mark 9:24). This prayer of honest fear is actually a prayer of deepest faith. Such a prayer assumes that God is there, even if we cannot feel or quite trust that presence. It assumes that God is not offended at our human doubt and fear, that God *longs* to help us, that God *is able* to help us. It is a prayer that consents to God's act of inner healing, in spite of our fear. At the first utterance of our cry and our consent, God's radical healing moves to our deepest core.

**Four Suggested Meditations for
Deepening Our Trust in God:**

> For I, the LORD your God,
>   hold your right hand;
> it is I who say to you, "Fear not,
>   I will help you."
>   —Isaiah 41:13

> "Lord, I believe; help my unbelief!"
>   —Mark 9:24

Meditation One

As you relax your body, note, without self-judgment, your bodily areas that feel tense, defended, frightened. Your muscles are reflecting inner wounds of hurt and fear. You may wish to lay your hand gently on some of those bodily areas, or picture Jesus, the Healer, laying gentle hands on them. Rest, and quietly breathe, letting God's breath and God's light flow through your tight bodily areas: your facial muscles, your jaw, your back, your shoulders, arms, hands, abdomen, legs. Do not worry if there is not instant or complete relaxation. It is enough that you are here, willingly, in the presence of the Healer.

Now think of some experience of your life, either long ago or recently, that makes it hard for you to trust. Ask Jesus the Healer (in whatever way the Christ comes to you, through an inner picture, or a sense of light or warmth), to go to that place in time, to that inner hurt. Picture or sense the Healer defending, embracing, reassuring the frightened child within you. Let your inner fear be wrapped in a warm cloak of safety and protection, and be carried to a place of healing. What would such a place be like? Can you picture or sense it in some way? How is the frightened child within you comforted there?

Meditation Two

The first meditation may be enough for you at this time. But when you are ready to move on, here is another step of inner trusting:

> Bartimaeus, a blind beggar...was sitting by the roadside. And when he heard that it was Jesus of Nazareth, he began to cry out and say "Jesus, Son of David, have mercy on me!" And many rebuked him, telling him to be silent; but he cried out all the

more,...And Jesus stopped and said...
"What do you want me to do for you?"
—Mark 10:46-51

As you rest your body, start paying attention to your inner cries and needs that may be calling out in an outwardly negative way. If you feel that you have been critical, grumbling, worrying, complaining recently, look below the surface. Ask the Healer to call forth the inner need that is crying out. Take your time. Look and listen deeply and compassionately.

Who, or what, seems to come forth? Picture, or think about, the Healer, Jesus, looking at you, responding to your inner deep need, just the way he responded to blind Bartimaeus. Your inner need, your inner hurt is honored and listened to.

Is there a need below the need? Is there a deeper longing trying to come forth? What is it? Can you see or feel or express it clearly? Ask the Healer to help you hear and understand.

Tell your inner need and longing that you will try to listen to its *early* signals from now on. What are its early signals? Try to learn to pay attention to them before the inner need becomes so insistent.

Meditation Three*

When I go and prepare a place for you,
I will come again and will take you to
    myself,
that where I am you may be also.
        —John 14:3

Think of some future experience that makes you anxious: a difficult day of work ahead, a problem professional meeting, an emotionally stressful family reunion, a doctor's appointment, a demanding journey, a speech you must give, a hard decision to make.

Envision, or just ask, the Healer to go ahead of you to that future time and place. Think of, or picture, the Healer entering that room, that office, that vehicle, that house, that classroom, that hospital. Be very specific and literal about it. Think about, or inwardly picture, the Healer moving around the whole place, touching the walls, the furniture, windows, doorways, spreading warm light into every corner of that space.

Ask that when you get to that place in time, you will feel that warmth, that welcome and empowerment as you enter that space. Though you will still have problems to solve and decisions to make, the experience as well as the place will be saturated with God's light. It has always been held in God's love, in God's heart, but now you will be *aware* of the light, and you will sense a change in the response of others.

Meditation Four

> O LORD, thou hast searched me
> and known me!
> Thou knowest when I sit down
> and when I rise up;
> thou discernest my thoughts from afar.
> Thou searchest out my path and
> my lying down,
> and art acquainted with all my ways.
>
> If I take the wings of the morning
> and dwell in the uttermost
> parts of the sea,

even there thy hand shall lead me,
and thy right hand shall hold me.
—Psalm 139:1-3, 9-10

When next you are in the midst of a difficult situation: a committee meeting, a hurtful confrontation, a family quarrel, or any situation in which you feel overwhelmed, or powerless, inwardly pray; breathing deeply and slowly:

Living Christ,
I give this situation,
this room,
all of us here,
to you.
Take over all the way.
Fill this room with your power.
Cover us with your light.
Take us fully into your hands and heart.
Transform us!

Notice what happens within you, around you, and with others when you pray this prayer of release. You will know that the age of miracles is not over!

*An expanded version of Meditation Three is found on the cassette tape by Flora Slosson Wuellner "Depth Healing and Renewal Through Christ," read by the author and produced by The Upper Room, Nashville, Tennessee.

Chapter Four

LEARNING TO LIVE
FROM OUR HEARTS

AS OUR ABILITY to trust is healed, as we let ourselves be increasingly bonded to and nurtured by God's heart, we begin to live more powerfully from our own heart center.

I think the whole purpose of my own life has been to learn to live from that center. As a child I was very closed off to the presence of others. It was not that I was loveless, but it did not occur to me to show much of that love, or to become intuitive toward the feelings of others.

How strange, as I look back, that God should call me into the ministry, long before I learned to show my love for the people around me! God has had much gentle work to do to open my heart's door.

Slowly, I still am learning what was once quoted to me (I do not know the source), "The head does not know anything until the heart has listened, and the heart knows today what the head will understand tomorrow."

As God continues to unfold me, I am increasingly fascinated by the faces, the body language of people I see on the streets, in airports, on buses. I am learning to see the signs of sorrow, endurance, burdens borne. I am learning to sense the presence of God saying through each person, "Here I am, coming again to you, giving myself again to you. It is I, encountering you through this person. The way you respond to this person is the way you are responding to me."

As I hear the life stories of others, I again sense the presence of God, through the living Jesus, suffering for, suffering with, abiding with, rejoicing and loving in each of these lives. I sense the awesome miracle of each life story. There has never been a story quite like this before, and there will never be one again. It is one of the major movements of living from our hearts when we begin to know and to feel the uniqueness of each other.

I wonder if this is part of the meaning of the temptation story of Jesus, when he struggled in the wilderness with the implications of his powers.

> The devil took him to a very high mountain,
> and showed him all the kingdoms
>   of the world....
>
> —Matthew 4:8

It is dangerous to see other people from "a very high mountain." When we see others from a far-off detached height, we forget to see them one by one. We forget to see them also as members of living communities, and, instead, see them as collectives. We are tempted to forget that we are one among them. We are tempted to manipulate others as functional parts of a large, impersonal whole.

If we are undertaking statistical analyses, it is

temporarily useful to see others in collective categories. But it is dangerous territory and is meant, at best, to be occupied only temporarily.

It is fatal, emotionally and spiritually, to start living and relating from that perspective. Increasingly, we become depersonalized and, also, depersonalizing to those around us.

As God opens our hearts, and as we begin to share more deeply God's heart, we learn to experience others face to face, person to person, as unique members of living communities, which is light years apart from the collectives that the tempter showed Jesus.

> And Jesus went about all the cities and
>   villages...
> preaching the gospel of the kingdom,
> and healing every disease and infirmity.
> When he saw the crowds, he had
>   compassion for them,
> because they were harassed and helpless,
> like sheep without a shepherd.
>   —Matthew 9:35-36

The "kingdom," the reign, of the good news is the polar opposite of the tempter's collective, faceless "kingdoms" seen from the high place. When Jesus, who saw from the heart, encountered the crowds, he experienced two things: each separate individual person *and* a living community.

> Are not five sparrows sold for two pennies?
> And not one of them is forgotten before God.
> Why, even the hairs of your head are all
>   numbered.
>   —Luke 12:6-7

The heart never lets the uniqueness and precious-
ness of the individual be lost in a crowd.

But the heart also sees and experiences a
communal soul, a communal body, with its own
history, its wounds, needs, empowered gifts. Many
politicians, teachers, ministers, actors have keenly
sensed a *group* feeling, a group need—question, hurt,
longing—rising powerfully from a communal gath-
ering. "I can almost see this group spirit coming forth
to meet me in its own body," one minister said to me.

I think, for example, that the dark, cold, rock-like
pain I saw around the living Jesus in that inner vision
in 1990 was no one individual's pain, but the agonized
spirit of humanity itself. It was vast communal pain.

It is important to realize that the awareness of a
communal presence is not a denial of the presence of
each individual member of the community. Both are
more deeply understood when we are aware of the
reality of both.

It is, undoubtedly, a deepening unfolding from
our hearts when we begin to see the wound in each
person, as well as in each community we encounter. A
man once told me that he was constantly on edge,
annoyed by his colleagues at his work place. He
increasingly disliked them, disliked the whole atmosphere. He was soon to retire, so it was not worthwhile
looking for other work. But what could he do in the
meantime?

I suggested he ask the living Jesus to walk down
the corridors of his workplace with him each day,
helping him to see the hurt within each person, each
with his or her own special burden or wound, often
carried defensively and silently behind surrounding
walls.

Recently, I read a description of one of the great
European cities, gripped by the bubonic plague, or the

Black Death, six hundred years ago. Houses in which anyone was ill were closed off, doors locked, windows boarded, guards set at the door until everyone in the house was either dead or well again.

Heartrendingly, the account described how one would walk down the city street and hear crying babies and children inside the boarded-up houses; children whose parents had died, who were alone, with no one to feed or help them. Sometimes one could hear the crying through the walls of an adjoining house, and it could go on for days. But few dared to break the law and dig tunnels through the walls to reach those children.

On any city street, on any bus, in any office, church, or store, we are surrounded by children in adult bodies, crying behind their defensive walls, inner children whose agony no one has yet heard. Or, those who heard their cries were either indifferent or unable to reach out to them because of their own inner pain and weeping.

I believe Jesus has heard this crying all the time: heard it from individual persons and heard it from hurting communal bodies. I believe Jesus heard it before ever coming into this world in human form, and that that is why he came to heal our wounds.

We do not help each other enough in our churches, in our spiritual groups, or in our religious teaching to distinguish between a sin and a wound. Although technically sin means "missing the mark" (and this could include every problem area in our lives), still, the word *sin* usually brings the association of guilt and self-condemnation. If we use *sin* to designate all aspects of our lovelessness and destructiveness, we may think that repentance, confession, and good resolutions will be enough. But if our problem has risen from a deep unhealed hurt, we need depth healing rather than just repentance and confession. I use *sin* only if there is free choice involved, some awareness of what we do, some space and time in which to choose. Destructive consequences of unhealed inner wounds usually rise so swiftly and overwhelmingly that we do *not* act in freedom. We *re*-act, rather than act.

I have often used the story of Peter denying Jesus three times in the courtyard of the high priest (while Jesus was held in secret trial) as an example of a hidden wound suddenly manifesting itself. Peter had never intended to deny his friend. He had sworn that he would never do this thing. But somehow, when the moment came, deep secret fear rose up and overwhelmed him. This was very different from the acts of Caiaphas and Pilate who knew clearly what they did and made a free choice.

When confession and repentance and good resolves do not change a problem, it is likely that we are dealing not so much with a sin as with an unhealed wound.

Considering the intense focus of Jesus on individual and communal pain, it is amazing that in our average church service we always find the confession of sins, but almost never equal time and place for awareness and sharing of unhealed wounds!

As we grow and mature in God's heart, we begin to hear the crying child within us, around us, whom God embraces. A significant dream was once shared with me. The person dreamed he was flying, in ecstatic joy, toward the sun. But in the midst of his flight he heard weeping far below. Looking down, he saw a dense green forest. Among the dark trees, he could see many people groping their way, crying desolately. He turned in the air and flew down to the forest.

Was this dream a vision shared from the heart of the living Jesus? Was it a guiding, prophetic dream about the person's own life? I believe it was both. Sometimes we hear the silent weeping around us before we have learned to love God. Sometimes we hear it *because* we love God. But in either case, we hear it because God's heart speaks to us directly.

Responding to that heart from our heart, we feel less the cold, manipulative expedience offered by the tempter, who from the high mountain, "showed him all the kingdoms of the world and the glory of them." Now we hear the *cries!*

I love you, Lord Jesus, because of the multitude who shelter within you and whom, if one clings closely to you, one can hear with all the other beings murmuring, praying, weeping.[1]

This vision, this hearing from the heart, is not a denial of the need for the anger that cleanses or of the need for our own strong borders as we reach out in love, or of the necessity of sometimes saying no. The next two chapters will explore these necessities as a vital part of living from our hearts. This growing ability to hear the surrounding cries is not the same as sentimental indulgence or weak submissiveness to the will of others. We are reflecting here on the gift from God, both extremely painful and extremely joyful, of the sensitivity to the wounds of others. And this special sensitivity will be mingled with, matched by growing power and freedom, the only healthy ground of love.

[1]Pierre Teilhard de Chardin *Hymn Of The Universe* (London: Collins, 1971), p. 69.

Another profound step in the life unfolding from the heart is to see the deep radiant being within the other person. Think now of the person you dislike the most. Do not try to force yourself into love or even liking. Just imagine this person healed, released from suffering, released from fear. Imagine this person awakening from moral sleep, learning to love, to make decisions. Imagine this person released from some inner imprisonment, able to trust, knowing himself or herself loved and held precious. How would this person's face change? What change would come into this person's voice? How would this person begin to relate to others, to you? Now think of this person released fully by the radiance of God into his or her special gifted power, the inner wings unfolded, living the life for which he or she came into the world.

Can you begin to sense the radiance, the light within the other? Even to hear the pain of another is already a strong intercessory prayer. To sense the light-filled person within the other is an equally powerful intercessory prayer. Just to be aware of it (perhaps not necessarily *saying* it) can change a whole relationship, and bring new healing into the atmosphere.

This is, perhaps, how Jesus saw Peter in the fear-wounded Simon. Surely this is how the risen Jesus saw Paul within the fanatical persecutor Saul. This is how the living Jesus sees each of us!

The shining empowered one within ourselves is even harder to encounter than is our own inner woundedness. Perhaps we are afraid of becoming proud, arrogant. Perhaps we fear that we, too, will be taken up to that "high mountain" and tempted to manipulate others as collective crowds. Perhaps we do not yet understand that God's creation involves the ecstatic wedding feast as well as the foot washing.

What *can* we do when Jesus looks us in the eye and says: "You are the light of the world"? (Matt. 5:14) I wish I knew. I am still trying to deal with that!

Perhaps it is enough, at this point, for most of us just to say to God: "I hear you. I don't really know what it means, though. But I pray you to keep on seeing my inner empowered light, to strengthen it in me, to release it within me, more each day."

If we should pray frequently for our inner shining one, as well as our wounded child, we may discover that, deep down, they are the same! What radical change would then begin in our lives?

Perhaps, above all, our deepening vision from our hearts sees the goodness of just being human. A wise student once said to me, and I have quoted it with delight ever since, "We are not so much human beings trying to be spiritual, as we are spiritual beings trying to be human!"

When she said this, my mind and perceptions did a kind of somersault, and lots of things fell into place! Something deep in me shouted, "Yes!"

Our humanity, though desperately in need of healing, is good in itself. It is not just something to rise above, just as the body of this earth is not a prison of the spirit or just a stepping stone to heaven. Our humanness is a beloved end in itself. So also is this earth beloved in itself. What a miracle it is to be a human being, in this mysterious, profound inter-mingling of the energy of spirit, and the no less holy energies of matter. What a miracle, to be on the frontier of this three-dimensional, five-senses dimension of creation! From Genesis to Revelation, the Bible glories in it.

Jesus' stories are all warmly human. He tells about the healthy daily activities of planting gardens, sowing fields, making bread, earning money, looking for lost sheep, getting married, having a baby, family quarrels, family celebrations. We can almost see him as a little child, then a young man, living in a village, observing and hearing all these holy acts of being simply human. We love clowns and comedians because they lovingly celebrate the warm absurdities and paradoxes of being human. Our deepest, most healing laughter wells up from the ludicrous, tender vision of these endless ways we fall over our own big feet.

There is a book I have loved for forty years. It would be one of the first things I would grab if the house were on fire. It was written in 1949 by J.B. Priestley, a famous English author. The book's title is *Delight*. Often he dealt with serious themes, but in this book he writes brief sketches about the little things, the human things, that have given him special delight all his life: reading detective stories in bed, hearing the sound of a football being kicked, old photographs, fountains, mineral water in bedrooms of foreign hotels, the smell and feeling of wood, suddenly doing nothing at all, being solemn about one's tastes, being recognized, making stew, orchestras tuning up, departing guests, seeing the flashes of three lighthouses from his window, and so on. I am sure this book has influenced me more, taught me more about happiness and the goodness of being human than most of the solemn books I have ever read (or written!).

The same deep joy in the small things of being human and of this earth, and the discovery of their holiness was expressed ecstatically three hundred years ago by another beloved writer, Thomas Traherne, an Anglican priest:

> Your enjoyment of the world is never right, till every morning you awake in Heaven,...and look upon the skies, the

earth, and the air as Celestial Joys....

You never enjoy the world aright, till the Sea itself floweth in your veins, till you are clothed with the heavens, and crowned with the stars:...Till you can sing and rejoice and delight in God, as misers do in gold... you never enjoy the world....

It was His wisdom made you need the sun. It was His goodness made you need the sea....

To have blessings and to prize them is to be in Heaven; To have them and not to prize them is to be in Hell....

Suppose a river, or a drop of water, an apple or a sand, an ear of corn, or an herb: God knoweth infinite excellencies in it more than we: He seeth how it relateth to angels and men; how it proceedeth from the most perfect Lover to the most perfectly Beloved, ...and for this cause it cannot be beloved too much. God the Author and God the End is to be beloved in it; Angels and men are to be beloved in it,...O what a treasure is every sand when truly understood! Who can love anything that made too much? What a world would this be, were everything beloved as it ought to be![1]

So many false and dangerous forms of spirituality have been taught through the centuries which deny, repress, constrict this free vision of delight in the earth and in humanity.

The opposite of the divine is not human. Rather, the opposite of the divine is the *inhuman:* that which scorns, condemns, fragments, and depersonalizes the human.

[1] Thomas Traherne, *Centuries Of Meditations.* Edited by Bertram Dobell. (London: P.J. & A.E. Dobell, 1950), pp. 19, 30–31, 122.

According to the ancient traditions, Lucifer was the angel of light who thought the whole risk of the human creation was a bad mistake, and who set out to prove to God what a worthless creature the human being is. There are many forms of spirituality subtly (though perhaps unconsciously) reflecting this view.

But as we live from our heart, bonded to Christ's heart, we see the body of this earth, not as a machine to be manipulated or a possession to be exploited, but as a living being to be treasured, a priceless reservoir, a cradle, warm ground in which our humanness is planted, rooted, nurtured.

Something else begins to unfold for us as we live from our hearts. We begin to discover the meaning of comfort, God as the Comforter, ourselves, letting that warm wind blow into and from our hearts.

Comfort does not mean the same thing as anesthesia. Nor, in the biblical sense does it necessarily mean the same as comfortable. It is a living power. Comfort comes as a mighty presence; a strange, pervasive peacefulness in which we feel both energized and yet calmed, relaxed, but resuscitated.

When Jesus talked to his friends at supper the night before his death, he promised to send them the Holy Spirit (John 14:16, 26). The word which describes the Holy Spirit differs according to the particular translation of the Bible one reads. In one translation, the Holy Spirit is called "the Counselor." In another, "the Advocate." In yet another, "the Helper." All of these designations are true. Yet, though usually I prefer the new and clearer translations of the Bible, the King James Version uses a word for the Holy Spirit which, for me, is the most powerful of them all: "the Comforter."

The power of this designation came to me not long ago when I was awake one night hurting and worrying over dear friends of ours who were in a critical and traumatic emotional crisis in their lives. I could not think of any practical way to help them. Ordinary prayer did not seem to be helpful this time. I just lay awake, staring in the darkness, my heart racing.

Then, slowly and powerfully, inner words were given to me. I am not usually a *word* person in prayer. I usually find inner picturing more helpful, or an inner sensing or feeling, or bodily prayer in which I breathe each breath, knowing it is God's breath breathed in me, or laying hands on my heart, or looking at and maybe holding a special object. But this time it was most definitely *words*, words that came as if someone were saying them for me until I began to say them. It seemed important that I say them very slowly:

"Holy Spirit…Comforter…Breathe on them now…"

I repeated this prayer, several times, with perhaps a pause of a full minute between each phrase. After a while, the prayer changed to:

"Holy Spirit…Comforter…Breathe on *us* now…"

My own breathing now was slower and calmer. I laid my hands on my heart, until my whole chest and heart area felt warm. The prayer seemed to become part of my breathing, part of my body.

Finally, it spontaneously shifted to:

"Holy Spirit…Comforter…Breathe on me now…"

By this time I began to fall asleep, deeply comforted.

This does not always happen, but when I saw my friends the next day, a miraculous change had occurred between them. A healing and reconciliation had happened that I had not thought remotely possible.

Then I remembered two biblical passages, which in the confusion and distress of the night I had not thought of at all, even when those powerful prayers came to me.

> On the evening of that day...
> Jesus came and stood among them
> and said to them,
> "Peace be with you.
> As the Father has sent me,
>   even so I send you."...
> He breathed on them, and said to them,
> "Receive the Holy Spirit..."
> —John 20: 19, 21, 22

> The Spirit helps us in our weakness;
> for we do not know how to pray as we ought,
> but that very Spirit intercedes
> with sighs too deep for words.
> —Romans 8:26, NRSV

I believe that in my deep need, God's Holy Spirit breathed on us all, just as the risen Jesus breathed the comfort and power on his friends. I also feel that the same Spirit of comfort prayed for me in my distress, with prayer far deeper than words, giving me words that came directly from the Healer's heart.

Meditation

Think of some person whose problems distress you. Relax your body, breathing God's Holy Spirit, the

breath of life. Ask that the eyes of your heart open.
Remember God's promise to God's beloved people.

I will...put a new spirit within them;
I will take the stony heart out of their flesh
and give them a heart of flesh.
—Ezekiel 11:19

Ask to begin to see or sense the hurt, the unhealed
wound, or heavy burden within the other. Do not
contrive any special feeling. Just begin to see and hear.

Sense or picture God's hands closing gently
around the wounded heart of the other, the way your
hand would close around a small, frightened bird,
warming and calming it.

Hold this inner picture or thought as long as
seems right. When and if you feel ready, ask to picture
or sense the radiant being of light within the other.
Picture or claim the power of Jesus, raising up the
sleeping beautiful empowerment of the other, the way
Jesus raised the little girl from her death-like sleep
(Mark 5:22-24, 35-43). Maybe some other image comes
to you of the awakening and released happiness and
giftedness of the other person.

If the inner picturing seems difficult for you, ask
God's Holy Spirit to give you a special word or words
to use when you think of that person, such as the one
given to me:

"Holy Spirit...Comforter...
Breathe on (___give name___) now!"

When you feel ready to pray for yourself, lay your
hands on your heart. Identify the wound there.

Picture or sense God's hands, very gently cradling
your agitated heart, holding it like a frightened,

wounded bird. Just let your heart beat within that hand for as long as you need to. This can be an extremely powerful and healing form of prayer.

Does any special word or phrase come to you from a deep place; some word that you need to hear right now? Say the word or words over and over, very slowly until they become a part of you.

When you feel ready, pray for your inner light, your radiant child of God, even if it does not yet seem very clear or real to you.

> "Loving God, awaken my inner radiant one...strengthen my radiant one...release my radiant one within me...empower my radiant one...bond my inner light to your heart, forever."

Picture now the photo of the earth taken from outer space, that globe of blue, brown, white, green, and think of the words from scripture: "God so loved the world.... See, or think of, the hands of the Healer, gently holding the earth's body, again, as you would hold a beautiful bird, until the warmth and light of the Healer's hands penetrate to the center core of the earth. See, or think of, the warm healing light flowing outward to all parts of the earth body. Picture the Healer putting the beloved earth into his heart to be cradled, fully healed, transformed.

> For God so loved the world that he gave his only Son....
> —John 3:16, NRSV

Now sense, or think of, your own body, your own self, parts of this beloved earth. Picture your feet deep within the earth, the way you would bury them in warm sand. Let the warm strength flow up through your feet, slowly into your own body.

When you feel ready, slowly bring your attention back to your present surroundings. Stretch, gently rub your face and hands, and bring your meditation to a close.

Chapter Five

OUR ANGER AND GOD'S HEART

BUT AS WE LEARN to see and respond to the wound, the inner light, and the humanity of others, what do we do with our very human anger? Does it just vanish? Do we rise above it? Is it swallowed up by light?

I have had to learn a lot about anger as it relates to our love and our spirituality. In my early days of teaching and writing, I was certainly aware of its uncomfortable existence, but tried to push too quickly past it. I think I was still affected, more than I had realized, by much spiritual teaching that anger is the opposite of forgiveness, that anger is a non-spiritual reaction.

Recently I have been reading children's books and child-rearing manuals written in the last century. Children were not only forced to obey, they were forced to obey *cheerfully!* Any sign of anger, any feeling of rebellion, was punished as severely as was the naughty act. Parents were urged to ask a child to search his or her heart every evening before bedtime, and to confess any angry feelings there as if they were sins.

There is something of this same condemnation of

anger in the communion service many of our churches still hold, in which the invitation to communion depends on whether you are or are not "in love and charity with your neighbors." Probably the intention of this wording is to warn us against hypocrisy, taking the bread and cup when we are unaware of or indifferent to our neighbor's needs. But, unfortunately, many people interpret it as meaning that when we are angry with someone, we don't deserve to receive communion.

How many times do we hear (or preach) sermons exhorting the congregation to forgive and to love, without any guidance at all about just what to *do* with the reality of anger which is part of our humanity? As we are bonded increasingly to the heart of the living Jesus, what is the meaning of anger, what are the uses of anger?

There seem to be two major forms of anger. One is the murky, unclear anger, what I call "infected anger," in which we do not know clearly just why we are angry or at whom we are angry. We just know we *are* angry, more or less chronically. This kind of anger smolders within us, erupting and lashing out unexpectedly on inappropriate occasions.

One woman shared with me that every time she got angry, *all* the hurts and angers of her life instantly attached themselves to the present occasion like magnets. Her reaction, of course, was far more intense and overwhelming than the occasion justified.

Infected anger is extremely destructive to the bodily health and happiness of both ourselves and those around us. This type of anger fills the emotional atmosphere. If this anger is found on a communal level, often it is used by unscrupulous political or religious leaders to manipulate their communities, skillfully directing smoldering anger toward scapegoat

targets. Unclear, murky anxiety and fear (closely related to anger) is often manipulated in the same way.

In contrast, there is *clear* anger, which is the clean,
healthy flame of outraged justice and humanity. This
is the anger in which we know its cause and reason.
This anger can be a powerful, creative energy for defi-
ance of evil, for decision making, for protection of self
and others, and for limit-setting. It is out of this clear
anger that forgiveness and reconciliation from healthy
roots can eventually rise.

Jesus' anger was not a denial of love and healing.
It was the bright fire of God's own indignation. For
God is love, and when love or humanity is violated
and abused, clear anger is part of love's own health.

For example, Jesus expressed fiery outrage over the
abuse and exploitation of children (see Matthew 18:1-7,
10). But I believe his anger for the children's sake was
not separate from his equally fiery grief for the abuser.
Immediately following his denunciation of child
abusers, he tells this story:

> What do you think? If a shepherd has a
> hundred sheep, and one of them has gone
> astray, does he not leave the ninety-nine on
> the mountains and go in search of the one
> that went astray?...So it is not the will of
> your Father in heaven that one of these little
> ones should be lost.
> —Matthew 18:10-12, 14, NRSV

Certainly "these little ones" refer to the child, the
victim who has been abused. But does it not *also*
include the abuser who carries within him or her also
a desperately hurt child who was never comforted and
healed?

Recently I read a powerful remark by Swiss

psychiatrist Alice Miller, *"Every persecutor was once a victim."*1

There was a heart-rending example in the news not long ago. A young man kidnapped a child and kept her for several years, caring for her yet also sexually abusing her. When the child was eventually rescued and the young man arrested and tried, his own tragic childhood story was brought to light. His emotionally confused, weak parents had turned him over as a seven-year-old child to an elder man who enslaved him bodily and emotionally all through the young man's youth, alternately cherishing, punishing, depending on him, yet abusing him. He grew up, breathing that infected atmosphere, not knowing any other way to relate to people. This person, and others like him, must be confronted and stopped. Anger toward such an abuser is appropriate. But also, we begin to understand *why* someone might move into the role of an abuser, having known nothing else. Such abusive, addictive, destructive ways of relating can be passed down through generations, inherited, internalized, passed on to other innocent victims, pulling them into the web of evil in their turn.

God's love and indignation challenges us to confront and stop abuse of all kinds. But God's passionate loving search for *each* "little one" will never end, just as the fierce, loving search of the shepherd did not end until the sheep was found.

What then does the Bible mean by "hell"? Is there not a point at which God's love ends, in which the loving search is given up? Is there not a state in which God's anger has canceled out God's love?

There are two significant stories in the Gospels that

1Alice Miller, *For Your Own Good: Hidden Cruelty in Childhood and the Roots of Violence*, (Farrar, Strauss, Giroux.,1983), p. 249.

imply another interpretation. In the Gospel of Luke (16:19-25) Jesus tells the story of a sick, hungry beggar who sits at the door of a rich man, who ignores his needs. After the rich man dies, he begins to suffer deeply over his cruel neglect of the poor. He agonizes over the chance that his family will also repudiate God's love this way. God speaks through Abraham to the suffering spirit, calling the man "my son." In other words, though the rich man has violated love, has much to learn, and a long way to go, nevertheless, the relationship of parent and child still continues in God's heart. *Nothing* can break that bond. Hell is a condition of lovelessness and the refusal to be helped and healed. God does not send us there. It is a condition we have made for ourselves. It is a condition we make for others. God's heart longs to heal us of this dark, choking miasma, and to end our "hell," whether in this life or the next. But no matter how long we choose to stay in this fog, God still says to each of us, "my child."

In chapter two, I spoke briefly of Jesus' vision of the final culmination, in which those who have helped the helpless are divided from those who have ignored the pain around them, as the sheep are divided from the goats (see Matthew 25:31-46). Those who have ignored the cries of misery are sent into destruction. But it is made specific and clear that this challenge and judgment is made to *nations*, the communities: "Before him [the Son of man] will be gathered all the nations, and he will separate them one from another" (v. 32).

Nations, states, cities, churches, families that abuse or neglect the vulnerable will not survive as communal bodies. Many civilizations and nations have not survived. Communities will most definitely break up or become severely weakened if they lose their humanity.

But the individual soul, the "little one" will never be lost from God's heart.

These biblical stories help us understand the meaning and power of clear, creative anger over abusive injustice, and also to understand more fully the compassionate grieving within God's heart. This mingling will unfold in our own hearts as our own healing deepens.

I am impressed with Alice Miller's thoughts about anger and forgiveness:

> Forgiveness which is based on denial of the truth....is not true forgiveness....
>
> Genuine forgiveness does not deny anger but faces it head-on....Only if the history of abuse in earliest childhood can be uncovered will the repressed anger, rage, and hatred cease to be perpetuated. Instead, they will be transformed into sorrow and pain that things had to be that way. As a result of this pain, they will give way to genuine understanding, the understanding of an adult who now has gained insight into his or her parents' childhood, and finally, liberated from his own hatred, can experience genuine, mature sympathy. Such forgiveness cannot be coerced by rules and commandments; it is experienced as a form of grace and appears spontaneously when a repressed (because forbidden) hatred no longer poisons the soul. The sun does not need to be told to shine. When the clouds part, it simply shines. But it would be a mistake to say that the clouds are not in the way if they are indeed there.[2]

2Miller, pp. 248-249.

We may need counseling, therapy, or at least many in-depth talks with others, as well as honesty within ourselves to sort out our emotional issues, so that they become increasingly clear within us. For all of us, the facing of anger and the exploring of depth healing is a spiritual journey which we can experience through the enrichment, comfort, and empowerment of honest prayer. As our healing deepens, it will be possible, as Miller witnesses, to begin to see with compassion the heart of the one who hurt us. We will begin to be able to choose decisive action that both sets boundaries and yet reaches out searchingly.

But what about the early stages of anger, when we first encounter the violations and injustice? What about that stage *before* we can feel compassion, *before* we can make clear decisions? What do we do about the rage we feel?

When I was leading a retreat group in a meditation for the healing of memories, I suggested the participants envision the person who inflicted the wound (mother, father, sibling, relative, teacher, neighbor) as a wounded child. I urged them to see the other as the angry, grieving, frightened, lonely little boy or girl carried around for years within the adult body.

At the break, a middle-aged man came up to me for some private sharing, and asked: "But what exactly can I *do* with my anger? If I inwardly picture my father as a hurting child, then I can't appropriately let loose my full anger at a child in this prayer. That would be abuse on *my* part. I have no safe place to put the energy of my anger. It just turns inward and becomes depression!"

This gave me a lot to think about. I had always been careful to warn people not to rush past anger or to contrive reconciliation too soon. But I had not given suggestions for a place to send the anger. I shared this problem when the group gathered together. "How about sending the power of our anger into the body of the earth?" I asked the group. "Right down through our feet into the ground."

"No!" responded someone very firmly. "The earth is polluted enough. It does not need more burdens of that sort." We all felt she was right.

My inner vision of the heart of the healing Jesus which came to me a few months later has been for me a powerful answer to that question. Now I suggest to individuals or groups that they let their anger take some symbolic form: a bird, an animal, lightning, a rushing river, fire. If some of them are not comfortable with inner pictures, it is enough to let spontaneous words or phrases rise, or just to sense the feeling as a mighty bodily energy. Then I suggest that instead of letting the feeling aim for the other person, send it with full force into the heart of the Healer. The living Christ offers to take directly into his heart the full impact of what we feel. Held in that heart, which is strong and tender enough to take the complete momentum of our rage, our energies will not be destroyed but embraced, cleared, healed, and transformed into the creative power which can forgive.

There is an analogy here to the action of our bodily hearts, which take our blood from the veins, loaded with impurities, send it to the lungs for cleansing, and then thrust the renewed blood out through the arteries to bring nourishment to our whole bodies.

God is not afraid of our feelings, nor will God be destroyed by them. God has already entered into them and invites us to send them fully into the transforming Source.

I had a strange dream many years ago. In this

dream I was watching a person (I could not tell if it was a man or a woman) standing on the steps of a great temple and facing the east. It was dawn, with the sun just rising. The person I was watching lifted a cup of wine into the rays of the sun as it rose. In the dream I understood, or was somehow told, that this cup of wine contained all the wounds and sins of the world. When it was lifted into the sun's rays, all human pain and evil was returned to the compassionate Source of life, the Healer of the universe who would transform the offering. It was the task of this servant of the temple to celebrate this healing ritual every morning at sunrise.

I did not fully understand the dream at that time, but later I realized the dream was a metaphor of what happens in all intercessory and healing prayer, whether for ourselves or another. We are returning the full impact of human rage and pain and woundedness to that Heart of strength and tenderness.

Meditation

> Violence shall no more be heard
>   in your land,
> devastation or destruction
>   within your borders;
> . . . .
> for the LORD will be your everlasting light,
> and your days of mourning shall be ended.
> —Isaiah 60:18, 20

Claim the presence of God's love in whatever way is right for you. Relax your body, and gently breathe each breath as if it were God's breath of life breathed into you. Rest in God. Remember that you are free to leave this meditation at any point if it becomes too painful or threatening. You are free to change any words or symbols.

When you feel ready, ask Christ, the Healer, to guide you to some hurtful memory. If this is the first time you have experienced memory-healing prayer, you may wish to begin with a memory that is not too traumatic. Ask the Healer to go ahead of you into that place where the event occurred. The place itself, the very space, will need healing. Sense, or inwardly picture, how the Healer fills that space with warmth and light. Enter the space of the memory when it feels safe for you. Sit quietly with the Healer, or walk around, seeing the warm streams of light flowing into every part of the room, across the floor, ceiling, windows, furniture, doors. Breathe the new air of the space until you begin to feel peaceful and reassured there. This may be enough for this time. You can always come back later.

When you feel ready, ask the Healer to invite in the other person who was involved in your hurt. Picture or sense the other entering as the child.

How do you feel as the other person enters? Listen to your body as well as to your feelings. You are safe. Christ, the Healer, is there enfolding you and protecting, you. But you are free to leave at any point. God's love does not force us to enter or to remain in places of pain.

Now let yourself feel fully. Do you feel anger, bitterness, rage, grief? If so, do not contrive reconciliation. Your anger is there for a reason. Does your anger or grief feel focused somewhere in your body? In your heart? In your abdomen? In your face or hands? Behind your eyes? You may wish to lay a comforting hand upon your body, or think of the Healer gently touching you.

Let your feelings take a symbolic form: a bird, or an animal, or a color, or storm clouds, or torrential rivers, or anything else that is spontaneous for you. Let these feelings and their power flow directly into the heart of the Healer who stands there between you and the other person. Let them flow into the Healer's body as long and as forcefully as you feel the need. Let yourself express what you feel with words or images or tears. You may even want to draw what you feel.

This may be enough for one time. Perhaps later (maybe much later) you may be ready to let the child within the other person express also what he or she feels; to share her or his own woundedness, grief, anger, or fear. If it is still too soon for this, it is enough just to be willing to be in the same space with the other person of your memory, held by God, letting your feelings go directly into the heart of Christ.

As you move back to the present time and place, let the entrance to that door of the past remain open, so that its healing light will shine along your path of return. If you decide to go back to that place of memory at some later time, the healing will move to an even deeper place within you.

When you think of that other person, try to see the hurting child within him or her, also held by God's tenderness. This is a powerful and effective way to pray for our "enemy." We do not at any time have to force love or even liking within ourselves. Neither do we have to force the feelings of full forgiveness. It is enough to see the other person as also God's beloved child, held by God. Later, the feelings of forgiveness will come spontaneously.

Rest quietly again in God's presence, gently massaging your face, hands, and arms, becoming aware of the chair, the floor beneath you. When ready, open your eyes and conclude your meditation.

Chapter Six

LOVING WITHOUT BECOMING A VICTIM

AS WE ARE BONDED increasingly to the heart of Christ, how do we relate to others in deepening love without becoming exhausted or feeling like battlefields or dumping grounds?

Recently someone shared with me: "I have gone to two extremes in my life. As a child, and right through early adulthood, I was walled-off from others, remote, detached, not showing my feelings. It was important for me to have constant strong control over myself and my surroundings. My protective shell was very thick.

"Then, when I became a Christian, I wanted to learn love. I became *too* open and vulnerable to others, super-sensitive to their needs. As my walls melted, I didn't even have any *borders!* I now not only enter into every one else's pain, I also constantly take it into myself. I've lost all control over my time and energy. I feel pulled at and drained by others all the time!"

This story was very similar to mine. It is the story of many in the helping professions who are so beset by the problems and needs of others that their bodies and emotions are giving severe distress signals. Some have become numb. Chronically tired, they have become *disempowered!* How subtly and quickly this can happen when we have not yet experienced—or have lost—our healthy borders, and have so internalized the pain of others that we experience their symptoms in our bodies, in our emotional reactions, and even in our dreams.

But as Christians are we not to carry the painful burdens of others? We are, indeed, called by Christ to recognize this cross, in the particular way it comes to each of us, and to carry it. But our true cross involves our free consent, our free decision. It does not mean being invaded and drained. Our consent to our cross is meant to rise from an inner empowerment, not an inner helplessness.

Jesus freely chose his way each step of his life. When he was finally arrested, he knew he was not helpless, powerless. He spoke of the "twelve legions of angels" (Matt. 26:53), the awesome powers of protection, on which he could call if he chose. His decisions and his actions rose from inner freedom and power.

Living within God's heart, living in love should not turn us into helpless victims, either of others or of our own inner compulsions. In fact, the more powerless and victimized we become, the *less* we are able to love others fully and freely. If we have no control over our lives, no choices, we have become jellyfish, not lovers and healers.

God exults in our freedom, our empowered identities. Humility does not mean despising our selves, our needs, our gifts. Humility means the eagerness to learn, to keep growing, the willingness to receive and be helped by the love and gifts of others. Humility does not mean letting ourselves be trampled on by others with all control taken out of our hands. Rather, it means that we long for others to be set free, to be healed and empowered even as we are.

There are signs that we are becoming increasingly disempowered, whether by sharing others' pain without free choice, or by internalizing the pain of others into our own bodies and emotions, or through general lack of healthy borders and boundaries in our lives.

One of the first signs may be a chronic fatigue, when no organic reason for it has been found. Or there may be a sudden onset of exhaustion, along with symptoms of cold, dizziness, anxiety, depression, irritability—for which no medical reason can be found.

Or we may begin to feel in our own bodies the actual symptoms of those we are trying to help.

We may start dreaming about the problems of others.

We may feel anger or anxiousness out of proportion to what has actually happened.

Sometimes the disempowerment comes not so much from anything in our relationships or surroundings at the present time, but because we have *inherited* a sense of pain and woundedness from many generations. This is the form of suffering *that did not begin with us*, but is a family wound and burden into which we were born. I often remember and share the story that haunts me, of a family which had a widespread difficulty in expressing spontaneous emotions of any kind. The young woman who talked with me about it thought it may have stemmed from the childhood trauma of her great-grandmother who had been sent far away from her family and home when she was only three years old, to live among strangers. The little child who held down her feelings of grief, loneliness, and anger grew up to be a woman who could not trust or release her deep, spontaneous feelings. Therefore she found it hard to bond closely and emotionally with her children, who in turn passed on the same emotional constriction.

Resentment can be carried through generations. I read the poignant sharing of a man in his forties who was just beginning to understand how much he had been affected by the resentful anger and fierce competitiveness of the men in his family. It was no one incident, it was the very air he breathed all his life. Apparently, it had been the same for his father and grandfather before him.

These communal, generational wounds affect not only families, but communities of all kinds. I have talked with ministers who have experienced the special suffering and burden of a church community that has been hurting and dysfunctional for many decades. Such churches often do not know that they have inherited communal pain and problem. They usually blame the current minister, projecting the unarticulated problem and shadow outwardly. Usually there is a rapid turnover of ministers in such parishes, and these pastors may have experienced strange bodily symptoms and emotional depression.

"Every time I go into that church building," one pastor told me, "I feel as if a large, heavy, dark wet sponge drops on my head. I feel sick and depressed all the time I am in that building. I'm finding it hard to sleep and eat well, and all my dreams are restless and troubled!" This was a minister who was experienced and had previously served several parishes successfully. The church was troubled, wounded, and had been so for almost a generation. But the pain was not apparent to most members of the congregation. The problem was not shared openly. They thought they just had bad luck in pastors.

Is it this inherited communal pain of which Isaiah spoke when he witnessed to a special kind of healing?

> They shall build up the ancient ruins,
> They shall raise up the former
> devastations;
> they shall repair the ruined cities,
> *the devastations of many generations.*
> —Isaiah 61:4 (*italics* added)

Here are some signs that we may be carrying, perhaps unknowingly, communal shadow and woundedness which began before we ever entered the situation:

We may feel an inner hunger, an empty void at our very center core, which no amount of present love and nurture seems to fill. This is especially evident if it is a family unfulfillment which we shared and breathed in our early, formative years.

Another sign may be that prayers for personal healing do not seem very effective for us. Unconsciously we are trying to heal the woundedness of many people, perhaps of many generations, all in our own life.

Often we feel guilty when we *do* feel happy and free, as if we were betraying someone, or as if we do not deserve such good feelings.

Also, there is often a chronic anger or anxiousness which we cannot trace to any one main event in our lives. It has just been pervasive in the atmosphere around us.

Living from God's heart, how can we become open without being invaded? How can we give without being depleted? And, conversely, how can we claim boundaries and spiritual protection without building defensive walls? We certainly did not become

Christians in order to retreat back into our oyster shells!

Here are some suggestions that have helped me and others:

First, it is essential to be honest and discerning about the personal wounds and vulnerabilities still unhealed within us. At what points do we fall off the edge? Where do we become panicky? When does serious fatigue set in? What wounded child cries within us still? Have we begun to let God heal us at depth?

It is equally essential to be honest about the inherited wounds of our communities, especially if they are still an unnamed shadow side of the community.

It is vital to claim our freedom to choose just where and in what situations we are called to serve. God does not ask us to lift *every* cross. We are to lift our *own special cross*. We recognize our cross by the strong sense of authentic calling we feel (far beyond just the sense of duty), the joy alongside the suffering, the freedom of choice we are given, and the strength and grace we are given by God to carry it day by day.

I believe we are *not* called to a commitment or a community or relationship if we feel primarily a sense of duty and guilt, or if we have had a long history of disempowering co-dependence with this person or group, or if the sense of heaviness, darkness, depression deepens within us. Jesus spoke of the state in which "your [whole] body is full of darkness" (Luke 11:34). This can mean many things, but I believe one of its meanings is a sign that we are living a life not meant for us, not right for us.

If we have chosen to enter, share, and help lift the pain of another, it is essential that we be clear about our own human needs and limits. If we have over-extended ourselves, we tend either to keep on surrendering to the need of the other, or to go to the other extreme of abrupt withdrawal from the other. This can be extremely destructive if we have allowed the other to become dependent over a long period of time. It takes inner strength and clear honesty to admit our mistake, share our own need, slowly wean the other from constant dependence.

We need to be firm with ourselves and others about claiming a sabbath. We need to choose intentional time at regular intervals for rest, recreation, and renewal. This would not be the time to catch up on intensive correspondence, heavy reading, or cleaning the basement. It would be the time to do something utterly joyful and delightful. Sometimes it is hard to believe that God really wants us to experience joyful relaxation and that such can be a sharing and bonding with God's heart, as deep as the sharing of pain. Neither should cancel out the other.

Dreams can be extremely pointed about this. Not long ago, I had overcommitted myself, was exhausted and emotionally absent from those around me. One afternoon I briefly fell asleep and had a short, vivid dream. In the dream, someone rang the doorbell. I ignored it. Then came a knock. I paid no attention. Next came a pounding so hard that it cracked the door panel. Looking angrily through the crack, I saw a small child smiling up into my face. "Come out and play!" he pleaded. I needed no Delphic oracle to interpret that dream. I took the next day off.

> Listen! I am standing at the door, knocking;
> If you hear my voice and open the door, I
> will come in to you, and eat with you and
> you with me....Let anyone who has an ear
> listen to what the Spirit is saying.
> —Revelation 3:20, 22, NRSV

This need for re-creative change includes what I call the mini-sabbaths—those moments when we stop, gaze out the window at something beautiful, stretch, breathe slowly and deeply, drink some water, envision and wrap God's light around our body.

While seeing students individually during office hours, one after the other, I learned how important it was for me to go out of the office, if only for a minute or two, between interviews. I would walk swiftly down the hall, drink water, wash my face and hands, open a window, and breathe deeply. This habit not only gave me a refreshing break, but it also cleared for me an emotional, spiritual space in which I could meet the next person freely.

On days when I did not claim these moments of clear space, my body and emotions would give increasing warning signals of impatience, nervousness, irritability, or heavy lethargy.

These spaces, these sabbaths, are the healthy borders we can claim for ourselves. All healthy creatures of God's creation have borders as part of the beauty and identity of each person and each object: the outline of trees and mountains against the sky, the clear delineation of each leaf and flower, the vibrant brilliance of one color alongside another color. Borders are also part of our strength and empowerment. One year I worked as secretary in a hospital surgical ward. I observed many operations, and I was struck how each organ within the human body has its own strong lining, its own border. Without these borders, our bodily organs could not serve their unique functions.

Borders are not at all the same as defensive armor. They are not rigid or impermeable. They are flexible, living, breathing, strong in identity, and able, as part of that strength, to give and receive nurture.

It is interesting, and a powerful spiritual metaphor

that the bodily heart, too, has four separate chambers. There is a firm wall of muscle dividing the right side, which receives the exhausted blood loaded with waste material, from the left side which sends forth the refreshed oxygenated blood out on its renewed journey through the body. The sides of the heart work in harmony, but have distinctly different functions and powerful boundaries.

Finally, know that it is God, not you, who is the Healer, the source. Let God, through the living Jesus, bear the full weight of the burden and pain. Envision or tell the suffering darkness you share with another to flow like a swift river into the heart of the Healer. Or, even better, turn directly to the living Jesus, and ask him to take that dark weight directly into himself. That mighty heart can hold it. You are there, not as the healer, not as a channel, but as a beloved companion of the Healer, helping to focus and intensify the presence of the Christ.

When I am working with the pain of another, listening, sharing, counseling, praying, I am enormously helped if I envision Jesus *between* me and the other person. Sometimes Jesus seems to kneel before the other, embracing that person or giving something to that man or woman. I am there as part of the loving, consenting community.

In this way, I am protected from internalizing the symptoms or pain of the other into my own body. I am also protected from the presumption of trying to become the power and authority figure in the other person's life.

I think that many of the problems of inappropriate sexual behavior among the clergy, and others in the helping professions, are due to the longing to unite with the suffering ones, to take on fully their pain and problems. Clergy sexual misbehavior is an extremely complex problem, and there is no single or universal cause. But certainly one of the factors is ignorance of the necessity of appropriate borders between persons professionally connected. If, in our compassion and longing to help, we try to melt the borders, become one with the other, we can move quickly into a dangerous situation of sexual involvement and over-dependence.

This does not mean that we are to go through life afraid of deep, loving warmth, or to refuse to let our hearts feel affection and pain. I wish I could remember who it was that said to me recently: "We are crafted to sail on high seas. If all is *too* still and peaceful, it may mean that we have never left the harbor!"

We are created to work with God at the outermost frontiers where healing and redemption meet pain. But we should never try to become the ultimate healer and source of life for others. And, above all, *we should never try to carry the cross of Christ without being deeply rooted in the heart of Christ.*

Otherwise, our hearts will break, harden, or become demonic in arrogance!

Meditation

> Thou, O LORD, art a shield about me,
> my glory, and the lifter of my head.
> —Psalm 3:3

Relax your body. Sense, or picture, the closeness of God through Jesus Christ, the Healer. Rest, as you breathe that light and warmth of the divine Presence.

When ready, picture or sense your personal "space" around you. How wide does it feel? How high?

Are there colors? Does it feel like a room? A garden with plants and flowers? A mountain? A meadow, forest, lake? Or does it feel or look like something else?

Take a while to walk in your personal space, to explore it, to rest in it. This is your sanctuary, your own holy place. God sustains it, affirms and honors it, shines within it, breathes freshness through it. Breathe its air.

Does your space, your special place have borders? What do they look like? Are they beautiful? Strong? Clear? Do they feel rigid? Defended? Violated in some way? Or are they there at all? Do not condemn yourself. Just quietly note what you feel about your borders.

When ready, invite the living Christ, the Healer, into your space to help you explore and understand it. As you look around, do you feel or seem to see that someone or something (not necessarily evil) has entered your space and taken root there without your knowledge and consent? Does this intrusion seem to be recent or long ago? What effect is it having upon you? Does it drain your energy? What does it look like? A plant? Some other shape?

Ask Christ, the Healer, to speak to it and ask it its name. If it does not feel right to you that it should be there, ask the Healer to uproot it, gently and firmly. Ask the Healer either to carry the intruder out of your space to its own place, or to put it in the Healer's heart.

Ask the Healer to put something else in the place of the uprooting, some symbol of new life: a tree, a shrub, a fountain, a deep spring of water, a color, or some other living newness in place of that which has been taken away.

Explore your borders again. If they have been non-existent, weakened, broken so others can enter without your knowledge and drain your strength and being, then inwardly picture or claim the healing Christ coming with full power *between* you and anyone who drains you.

Picture the thirsty mouth (or roots, or tendrils) of the other going directly into the heart of the Healer where it will be nourished. God's heart can carry the full power of that need. This will free you to be near the other with love without being depleted.

Do you feel that *you* sometimes drink or drain from another person's energy without their consent, or that you intrude on their personal space in a way that depletes them? If so, sense or picture *your* thirsty mouth, hands, roots, directly connected to the heart of the Healing Christ, drinking in God's light and strength.

Or sense or picture an umbilical cord connecting your body with the heart of Christ. See how the healing light flows through the cord directly from Christ's heart to yours. Jesus spoke of the way we can drink our fill from his springs of life and strength:

> Those who drink of the water I will give them will never be thirsty. The water that I will give will become in them a spring of water gushing up to eternal life.
>
> —John 4:14, NRSV

When ready, inwardly look around and sense your space again. Does your space seem filled, saturated with a heavy family wound or with some other deep communal wound? Have you been carrying this burden in your body, your heart, your personal space for a long time? If so, and if you are ready to enter into prayer for healing and deliverance, claim the empowered light of the living Jesus Christ strongly around you, protecting you. Let the Christ invite the wound of your family or community to come forth in a symbolic way: a hurt child, a bird, an animal, a plant, a color, a shape, a group. As the communal pain comes forth, the Healer Christ opens arms and takes that group pain fully into his heart. Then the Healer folds sheltering hands over his heart, comforting, transforming.

If you are ready to be released from this heavy weight, sense or picture the hands of the Healer forming new and powerful light around your body, around your personal space. Feel the new light covering your broken, drained areas with new radiant substance. Let the light become itself powerful borders for you.

Ask the Healer to place a powerful, radiating light in the core center of your space. It can be warm or cool, radiating outwards, cleansing and refreshing your space, and creating strong, flexible borders.

Rest quietly, and breathe in the new air of your intimate space around you. Do you notice or feel any change?

Think ahead to a time when you may encounter persons or a group who have, in the past, invaded you or drained you of strength. Picture them also surrounded by God's light, with their own borders strengthened and renewed, breathing and drinking in the light from the heart of Christ. How do you feel your relationship with them will change?

When ready, bring your attention back to your body, the chair and the floor beneath you. Rest quietly, and let the new freshness of your cleansed space and the power of your inner light flow like a river to all parts of your body. Think of your bodily parts—every organ, every cell—eagerly drinking, soaking in this refreshing river of light.

Stretch. Gently rub your hands and face; and close your meditation.

Chapter Seven

WHEN GOD SEEMS ABSENT

SOMETIMES IT FEELS as if God is really absent. We feel no presence, no closeness. True, in our heads we may know that God never goes away. We feel as we do when thick clouds cover the sun. We know the sun is there, but we feel darkened and chilled.

"I was so happy feeling God's closeness for so long," a friend recently shared with me. "But now, there's just a big, empty void. I wonder if I have done something wrong and am being punished. Or maybe God is testing me to see how well I hold up!"

Another friend once said to me sadly: "I have *never* felt the presence of God. I hear other people talking about their wonderful experiences, but nothing like that has ever come my way. Maybe God doesn't love me as much as he loves them. Maybe I'm just not the spiritual type."

What is the meaning of such a sense of absence? *Does* God, after all, sometimes withdraw closeness? Is it because we have sinned, or disappointed God in some way? Does God intend for us to grow stronger and wiser because of this inner loneliness? Does it really mean we may be less spiritual than others? Is there anything that can be done about this condition, or are we supposed just meekly to endure it? Or should we start some strict, rigorous spiritual disciplines?

Like everyone else, I have gone through such times. Everyone I have ever talked to, even great spiritual leaders, have experienced the spiritual sun going behind the clouds. Likewise, some of the best people I know have only rarely felt a sense of the closeness of God. And we all inwardly ask the same questions.

For myself, I have come to some basic conclusions about the experience:

First, I am convinced that God, as we see God through Jesus, *never* leaves us, never withdraws or hides. I do not believe God either punishes or tests by removing the closeness. We are in a love relationship with the Holy One, not a manipulative liaison, not military obedience, not sentimental whimsicality.

"I will never leave you nor forsake you" (Heb. 13:5; Isa. 49:15-16a) is the essence of the scriptures. The clouds that seem to separate us from God's love are on *our* side. God has not willed them there.

Second, though the clouds are on our side, not God's, the separation we feel may not necessarily have anything to do with sin or being "un-spiritual." There can be many reasons.

We may be experiencing deep fatigue through stress, over self-extending, lack of nurture and recreation, or some bodily imbalance. The fatigue may be so deep-seated that we have lost much of our ability to feel or sense anything keenly. We need to ask ourselves if this emotional anesthesia is affecting only our relationship with God, or is it actually affecting many aspects of our lives. If so, it could well be fatigue even deeper than the usual symptoms of tiredness.

Or, we may be experiencing the presence of some

unhealed wounds that are making it hard to love, to respond, to trust.

We may be internalizing the problems or the heavy depression of others around us: some individual to whom we are close or some community to which we belong.

We may be experiencing the natural ebb and flow of feeling and awareness. These seasons of the spirit are natural in many aspects of our lives. Our awareness, our vitality, our ability to respond changes through the year, the month, the day. We each have a unique rhythm of cresting and quiescence.

Perhaps we need to explore new ways of being with God. Former ways of prayer may no longer be adequate for our new needs and our new growth. In every relationship, the time comes when new frontiers of being together need to be explored. Those who have never felt God's closeness may, possibly, have not realized all the exciting alternative ways of praying and listening to God. They may have experienced only the average Sunday service, and thought that was all—or enough.

Third, I am convinced that even though, at this particular time, we may not be able to feel God's closeness, nevertheless, God is not only with us but nurtures and sustains us each moment. Even when the sun is behind clouds, or it is night, the unseen rays are still giving life to the earth.

A fourth vital point is that God longs to restore our sense of closeness even more than we do.

This feeling of absence of God's presence, this dryness of the spirit, is not evil. It is not something to dread and fight against. Some people advise just restful quiescence, peaceful waiting for the spiritual winds to blow and the fog to lift. For myself, I suggest a more active, alert response. The following suggestions for the renewal of our awareness of God's closeness are not the same as contrivance of appropriate feelings, but they do seem to help clear the space, prepare the way, attune our attentiveness, heighten our sensitive response to God, who loves us.

Perhaps the best place to be in is to search our lives for any condition that is draining us, feeding on our vitality, lowering our energy to the point that it is hard to feel anything. You may wish to reread the previous chapter on loving without being victimized and fragmented. You may well find a connection between inner exhaustion and the loss of the awareness of God's closeness.

Another place to look is at our unhealed wounds, the traumatized trust, the unclear anger, the submerged grieving. Such wounds can surface unexpectedly and blot out the light of God for us. These are the issues explored in the chapters on trust and anger (chapters three and five).

A third suggestion is to try new ways of praying, relating to God, not grimly as if to force a feeling, but with expectancy and anticipation. You may wish to try alternating between a regular, intentional time of prayer and a more spontaneous approach. You will move from one to the other with refreshed joy. It is deadening (for me, anyway) to pray the same way all the time.

Let your body help you. Our bodies will be spiritual guides and friends if we will let them. Our bodies are in touch with our deep subconscious selves, through which God speaks more clearly than to our conscious minds.

For example, let your body move during prayer if that feels comfortable to you. You may want to walk around, kneel, take a few dance steps, stretch, hug yourself, raise your arms, lay loving, healing hands on yourself. You may want to sing, laugh, cry, speak aloud certain words or phrases.

Or you may want to take what I call a "parable walk," in which you take a walk without an agenda and see what God is personally telling you through the shape of a tree, a cloud, a dog, an ant, a bird, someone's face, a window, a color, a fragrance, a touch, a sound. There is always something you will experience, no matter in how small a way, which has significance for you.

Or you may want to write a letter to God, a totally honest letter, as you would write to the friend you trust most. Tell everything you feel in this letter to God, including your doubts about God and your anger.

Or set a chair in front of you, and ask Jesus, the Risen One, to sit there. Talk to him, inwardly or aloud, sharing your needs and feelings and longings. Then sit silently and see what seems to come to you inwardly. If nothing seems to happen at this time, keep alert the next few hours and days to see what changes come into your life. Usually what happens is very unexpected.

While you pray or meditate, hold in your hands a special picture or object that reminds you of God. Holding it against your heart may be a powerful experience. A friend once loaned me a beautiful copy of an Eastern Orthodox icon. (These can be found in many religious bookstores.) I laid it against my heart and just sat quietly, not picturing or asking anything. I was astounded at the river of energy and love that seemed to flow into my heart from the picture of the Christ. There came a feeling of direct communication that I had not experienced in many months. Such pictures are looked upon, by those who paint and pray with them, as open windows through which we look at God and God looks back at us.

But the object you hold need not necessarily be a picture. It can be a book, a cross, a pebble, a flower, a piece of cloth--anything that has strong associations for you with the love of God, and thus has become a sacramental object of us, through which we feel the healing current of the presence of the Healer.

Another suggestion is to choose some aspect of this miraculous creation to study and to reflect upon: some part of the human body, perhaps, such as the eye, the brain, the hands, or one of the vital organs. Or really study, or think about the structure of a tree, a plant, a mountain, a molecule, the atomic structure, a star.

A sense of almost overwhelming awe grows in us as we deeply contemplate the exquisite intricacy, balance, intelligence in each aspect of the body of this universe. Such wondering awe and delight is a deep act of prayer, a response to the intricate, guiding intelligence and divine unity from which each particle has grown. Nature is *not* the *same* as God. Our natural world is a creation, "groaning in travail," (Rom. 8:22) as well as rejoicing. But God's heart, God's spirit dwells within each particle, guiding, suffering, revealing an almost unimaginable purpose.

Three university courses deepened my awareness of the intelligence, majesty, and purpose of God as much as any church service I had ever attended: my biology course when I first looked through a microscope at a drop of water; my geology course when I first learned how the mountains grew, how the forms of life developed and changed so that thought and love could be experienced by these bodies; and my astronomy course in which I first learned of the dance of the stars and experienced the mind-reeling glance at light years, galaxies, and the unexplored mysteries of the universe.

Perhaps my first experience of God's presence through the sacramental gift of the earth was when as a child I was drawn to a special tree, a vast and ancient oak tree in a meadow, not far from our home. I would visit it several times a week, just to sit under it and lean against it. I even have a vague memory of bringing flowers to put at its base. I did not analyze my feelings about that tree. I just felt when I leaned against it with closed eyes, that I was leaning against a powerful, tender friend. I felt strength and mystery flowing into me. Looking back, I am very sure that I was also experiencing the close, loving mystery of the God who made and loved both me and the tree.

If you are feeling a loss of the awareness of God's presence, one of the most helpful things to do is to learn about the lives of some of the great lovers of God through history. Or learn about someone who has been transformed by God in this present time. The person need not be a great saint or mystic. He or she could be some ordinary person (are there any *ordinary* persons?) whom you know, one who has experienced God and whose life has been changed through that encounter.

Be prepared for human faults in this person, but take note of what has changed in this person's life. Note his or her vitality, inner joy, passion and compassion for the suffering people of the world. Note the humor, the spontaneity the warmth of this person. Notice the effect he or she has on the lives of others. How do you feel when you are in this person's presence?

There is a young woman I have known for many years. For a long time she was confused, angry, restless. Somehow, she found God's heart and was able to respond to that heart. I hardly recognized her when next I saw her. No sense of duty, philosophy, or good resolutions could have brought about such a change. Her life still has problems. I do not altogether agree with her theology. But she has emerged a full human being. The presence of Christ, the light of God glows through her eyes, and her choices, actions, and responses are brimful and overflowing with tenderness. I feel awed when I look at her! God's love is more miraculously revealed through the transformed human heart than through the stars or the atomic structure.

What sacramental experience of God comes to you through human relationships? Think now of the persons in your life whose love has comforted, empowered, nurtured you, believed in you, been there for you when you most needed it. Think of those who have helped you reach for your deepest self, whose love releases and does not constrict, who not only have compassion for your weaknesses and hurt, but who also *delight* in you.

Think about one special person whose love is there for you. Think about this person. Reflect and meditate on this person. Here again is God's presence. The way this person feels about you and responds to you, and reaches out to you is not only a miraculous reality in itself, but is also a hint, a taste of the way God feels about you—a million times more!

Now think about the persons *you* love most in the world. You long for their fulfillment and happiness. When they hurt you hurt with them. When they are happy you feel their joy at the very core of your heart. Sharing their burdens and problems does not feel like sacrifice, even when it is painful. You would rather be there sharing the pain with them than be off enjoying yourself with someone you love less. (I am speaking now of the persons you *really* love, not the ones you think you *ought* to love.) You are aware of their faults and weaknesses, but it has not the slightest effect on your love. No matter what they did, you would never abandon them. You also know that you cannot constrain or force their response. You would rather not have their response at all if it came forced out of obedience or duty or guilt. You want their love to be free and spontaneous, because they delight in you, as you do in them.

Meditate on your feeling about these persons for a while. Here is God's presence. The way you feel is a tiny taste, a faint shadow of how God feels about you and each one of us. We are made in God's image, the scriptures tell us. Therefore, we are able to taste, experience, manifest a slight measure of what God feels in an unlimited way about every particle of creation.

Think of an occasion when you felt a passionate longing to heal, to help, to comfort, to support. It may be linked with fiery indignation over injustice, greed, communal indifference, insensitivity towards the homeless, abuse of children and the elderly, neglect of the ill, abuse of the body of this earth (its soil, forests, water, atmosphere). You felt an energy flooding through you like a powerful river to involve yourself, to reach out, to become part of the transformation. Here is God's presence sorrowing, grieving, flaming, fighting through you! Here is God's impassioned heart, speaking directly to your heart. Here again, is the sacramental presence to be found, pulling you into the core of that love which hurts with every part of the hurting world.

Join with others, either with a committed group or one or two persons who are searching for a deepened experience of and encounter with God in their lives. Especially join with those who have already had some depth experiences of God's love. Be where they are. Talk to some of them and ask their help and prayers. Meet with them for prayer and sharing, on a regular basis if possible. The living experience of God is contagious!

Finally, choose one of the Gospels to read or reread. You might want to choose the Gospel of Luke which focuses with so much power on Jesus as the Healer. I have heard the fifteenth chapter of Luke called "the Gospel within the Gospels." If the rest of the Bible were lost, and we had only that one chapter, it would show us directly into the center of God's heart.

Read the Gospel you choose as if you had never read it, or even heard of it before. As you read, pay special attention to what Jesus says, and above all, to what he *does*. Reflect on the nature of God who is shown through this person. God is *like* this person.

How would the author of a book or play be able to communicate with the characters of his or her book or play, assuming they had the freedom to act and choose? Suppose the author knew the characters in the book could misunderstand or block the story he or she was trying to write? How would the author make clear the wonderful design of the story, or make clear what the author was really like?

Perhaps some of the characters in the book would be sensitively aware enough to communicate directly with the author, but most of them could not. Perhaps the *only* way the author could reach the characters would be to put himself or herself into the story as one of the characters. This person, written in, would enter the story fully, sharing the experiences of the story, relating to the other persons, speaking their language, undergoing the problems and some of the limitations of the dimension of the story. But, at the same time, this person, straight from the heart and personality of the author, would manifest to the other characters what the author was really like and what the author truly longs for.

Though expressing it in many different ways, Christians believe that this is what God has done through Jesus, in this drama of our world. "He [the Son] is the reflection of God's glory and the exact imprint of God's very being" (Heb. 1:3, NRSV). When God's presence seems distant, or absent, or unreal, focus on and cling to this miraculous personality, Jesus, who not only lived two thousand years ago, but lives now, still walking among us, reaching out to us, healing and empowering us. I have met and talked with many (some of whom are long-time trusted friends, some who are new acquaintances who share with me) who have seen the risen Jesus, who have seen his light, who have felt the healing touch and the warm power of that presence.

I had a strange experience some months ago during a semester when I was teaching. A student came for the first time to my office; a student of practical, down-right good sense, not given to "mystical experiences." Indeed, she was a bit doubtful of the reality of such experiences. As she came in, I noticed she hesitated a minute at the doorway, then sat down by my desk. We talked for awhile. She looked at me strangely several times, as if about to ask a question, but then would stop and go on to other matters. At the end of our hour, she said: "I need to ask you something very strange. I hope you won't think I'm crazy!" Naturally, I was fascinated, and I asked her go to on. "When I came in the door," she said musingly, "there was someone there—right at the entrance. That presence was so real, I almost bumped into it. Who was it, Flora?"

There was no way she could know that each time I was in my office, I asked the living Christ to be there, in a real and literal sense, not just as metaphor, not just as symbol, but as a real presence, so that all who came in would be touched by that peace and power. I myself did not always feel that presence. That day, for example, I was not particularly aware of it. And though I had often felt the inner peace flowing towards me, I had not felt it as a *bodily* presence in that office. But this student did. There was no way I could doubt what she said. As the semester went on, I often thought of her experience and felt my faith strengthened.

The living Christ walks among us, as real as when in the body. And even when we cannot actually feel that presence—as I did so long ago in that closet, and as my student did in the office—nevertheless, our lives undergo an almost unbelievable radical change when we commit ourselves, when we bond with that living being. Many of us need to *begin* with the loving commitment from which the deepening experience of closeness will flow, rather than wait for the experience before the commitment. It does not really matter which comes first. Every relationship with God's heart through the Christ is unique, as love always is.

This chapter does not conclude with a meditation, because each suggestion given is a meditative exercise. Others may occur to you by which you are able to open the door to the awareness of God more widely.

Perhaps the most important thing of all to remember is that all of these actions, exercises, reflections, are rooted in God's grace. We are not seeking a reluctant God who is hiding. Our very longing to feel closer to God exists because God already loves us, longs for us, has reached us, and spoken to us.

We love, because he first loved us.
—John 4:19, NRSV

Therefore, we can explore, experiment, try the new frontiers with expectant joy and confidence because, in fact, we are responding to the presence which has already and forever found us, the heart that holds us.

Chapter Eight

OUR FEAST, OUR CROSS, OUR FULFILLMENT

Christ in our hearts:
Passion of the Comforter.
>Pain mingling,
>Hands healing,
>Fire dancing,
>Bread breaking,
Blood and water, poured and flowing.

We in Christ's heart:
Beloved to the Lover waking.
>Bird soaring,
>Fish diving,
>Tree rooting,
>Child running,
Weeping hunger, finding, feeding.

Christ's heart, our hearts bonded:
Groaning of our earth, birth giving.
>Chains breaking,
>Light leaping,
>Eyes opening,
>Mountains singing,
Bride and Bridegroom, one cup drinking.

These words seemed to be written within me,
while I rested for a few days in a cottage beside a
small, radiantly blue lake in South Dakota, after some
strenuous teaching. I was also working on this book
and I was praying to be shown what happens within
us and around us when our hearts and Christ's hearts
are bonded. The images, the metaphors, came slowly,
as if rising from sources far deeper than conscious
thought. It was only later, when re-reading them, that
I realized every one of them is a biblical picture of the
love of God merging with the longing of our human
hearts.

The celebration of a feast is a major symbol, in
both the Old and New Testaments, revealing the tenderness, release, and transformation God intends for
us. These feasts—sometimes marriage celebrations,
sometimes honoring outstanding events in religious
history—included music, singing, dancing, and communal meals. Often they were accompanied by prayer
and sacrifice, the forgiveness of debts, and the release
of prisoners and slaves.

> He brought me to the banqueting house,
> and his banner over me was love.
> —Song of Solomon 2:4

> On this mountain,
> the LORD of hosts will make for all peoples
>   a feast....
> And he will destroy on this mountain
> the covering that is cast over all peoples,
> the veil that is spread over all nations.
> He will swallow up death for ever,
> and the Lord GOD
> will wipe away tears from all faces.
> —Isaiah 25:6-8

The LORD, your God, is in your midst,
a warrior who gives victory;
he will rejoice over you with gladness,
he will renew you in his love;
he will exult over you with loud singing
as on a day of festival.

—Zephaniah 3:17

It was at a wedding feast in Cana that Jesus was called to enact the first miracle of his love (John 2:1-11). It was at a feast in Jerusalem that he washed the feet of his friends and he shared the bread and wine, told them of his death and the coming of the Spirit. He told many funny, yet bitingly significant stories about feasts with tardy, reluctant guests, sleeping bridesmaids, feasts where people scrambled for the best seats. So much did he honor the feast as a time of human warmth, closeness, release, and the presence of God that he was criticized for his "eating and drinking" (Luke 7:34).

I visited Greece several years ago during Holy Week. On Easter Day itself we were in a huge, international hotel since we were to meet friends at the airport. We regretted we had to be in such an impersonal place, missing the experience of the true Greek Easter. But as evening came, we began to hear music, rhythmic, exciting folk music. Looking out the window from the eighth floor of our hotel, we saw, several stories below us, the flat, rectangular roof of a little apartment building. A large family was gathered there on the roof, preparing their Easter feast. Meat was cooking on a charcoal cooker. The delicious smells floated up to us. Pots of colorful flowers had been placed around the parapets of the roof. Rugs, cushions, and chairs provided cozy spots for rest.

While the meal cooked, the family members, all dressed in their bright, festal clothes, shared the homemade loaves of bread, the hard-boiled eggs, the jugs of wine. Repeatedly, various family members would start dances, circle dances, couple dances, solo dances. Sometimes it would be a grandfather or grandmother who would dance with a grandchild. Sometimes a young father would teach his little boys the right steps. Sometimes the teenagers would pull the grandmother or aunts away from the cooking into the dance. At one point, a young mother caught up her toddler in her arms and whirled into a dance with her. They were all completely absorbed in the fullness and significance of the moment, the Resurrection day, the sunset, each other, the music, the flavors of the cooking.

The feast lasted most of the night, and we didn't get much sleep. It didn't matter. As I watched, fascinated, I felt part of the heart of the feast. Also, I felt I was watching a scene whose roots stretched back thousands of years. This was, and still is, the way countless families have celebrated their feasts together. Jesus must have experienced so many of these rooftop festivals in Nazareth, Cana, Bethany.

Our communion service in church rises from the feast of Passover, the time of laughter, singing, bread-breaking, wine pouring, shared hearts, memories— and sacrifice. For the great feast was so inextricably mingled with sacrifice.

> If any want to be my followers, let them deny themselves and take up their cross and follow me.
>
> —Mark 8:34, NRSV

What does this mean? How does sacrifice, how

does self-denial fit in with a feast? How do they become part of Jesus' emphasis on healing, Jesus who said: "I came that they may have life, and have it abundantly" (John 10:10, NRSV). I do not believe that the call to deny the self and take the cross was said in a spirit of negativity and repression. It does not mean we are to dislike ourselves. On the contrary, we are to love our neighbors *as ourselves*. It does not mean we are to ignore our needs and wounds. Jesus never ignored anyone's needs and wounds. "Give us this day our daily bread," we are taught to pray in Jesus' own prayer.

Self-denial is not an end in itself, commanded by a God who likes to watch us suffer. Self-denial prepares the space for the feast of love with one another. We are to search with passion for our deepest longing—our inner, burning power to love as we grow within God's heart. And when we have found the great gift for which we came into the world, we are to let nothing interfere with its unfolding and release.

> The kingdom of heaven is like treasure hidden
> in a field,
> which someone found and hid;
> then in his joy, he goes and sells all that he has
> and buys that field.
> Again, the kingdom of heaven
> is like a merchant in search of fine pearls;
> on finding one pearl of great value,
> he went and sold all that he had
> and bought it.
> —Matthew 13:44-46, NRSV

There is self-denial in these two stories, a release of all that would interfere with the central, burning joy and love. This includes not only outer interference, but even more so it includes the inner interference of superficial desires, timidity, inertia.

Our cross is our free consent to commit our great inner empowered gift to help lift the pain and sorrow from the world, to share in the bringing of God's healing. This cross, our central vocation, brings joy, but it also brings genuine suffering: the pain of deepening sensitivity to others, the pain of letting go that which is extraneous, the price of much time and great energy expended, the risk of being vulnerable and misunderstood and sometimes hurt, and the on-going problem of saying no to that which would block us in our deep calling.

This denial, this cross, this saying no to that which blocks us and points out a more superficial way, does *not* mean ignoring the resistance within us. We are to listen with compassion to our hesitancies and fears. We are to be aware of the other needs and wishes which try to take control of our lives.

We are to listen lovingly, to bring our fear, our need to God's heart for healing and fulfillment. But fears and needs should not control our deep, central vocation and longing. Jesus listened to Bartimaeus and healed him, while on the way for the last time to Jerusalem. But he would not have permitted Bartimaeus to stop his way, any more than he permitted Peter to stop him. In fact, the story tells us that Bartimaeus, when healed, followed Jesus on his way (Mark 10:52).

This denial rises not from judgmental repression, or constricted living, but from the heart's center. It rises from our love, not from lovelessness.

When asked about marriage, Jesus quoted a significant remark from Genesis. I believe this quotation has implications for this understanding of our commitment to love: "A man shall leave his father and mother and be joined to his wife" (Matt. 19:5).

What a strange, radical thing to say! In Jewish culture at that time, one's duty to father and mother was considered to be paramount. It was one of the Ten Commandments. To deny a parent anything, short of a sinful act, was considered inexcusable. But Jesus tells us that God's will is that our core commitment must be to our spouse. I believe we can find here, even deeper than an interpretation of marriage, an insight into the central light within our hearts. That central love for which we leave all that holds us back can mean not only an actual spouse but also our cross, our feast; the new creation; the central shining gift for which we came into the world.

We experience our fulfillment, the fulfillment which God longs for us, when we find our cross and our feast together, one and the same, one unfolding to the other in the central fiery joy of our heart's love.

It is made clear throughout scripture that God longs for the *whole* creation, as it awakens to meaning, to the suffering and joy of love, to enter this fulfillment, this marriage feast. One night recently I awoke suddenly, thinking with amazement, *So that is what the sacrament of the Lord's Supper is all about!* Something I had apparently been struggling with on a subconscious level suddenly became clear as I slept. Almost all Christian churches, though widely differing in their way of expressing it, agree that Jesus Christ is present in some special and transforming way when the bread is broken and eaten, when the cup is poured and shared.

Some believe that Christ is present spiritually. Others believe that Jesus is also present bodily. Some believe that the bread and wine are transformed into the risen body of Jesus. Do we really differ basically? What do we mean by a "body"? A body is a manifestation of spiritual presence and energy within this three-dimensional universe, perceptible to our five senses. In a radical and mysterious way, Jesus in his risen body of light reaches out and unites with us when we share that bread and that cup in his name, binding us to him and to one another within that heart, within that risen body. I believe that exactly the same radical transformation happens when we enter into prayer in Jesus' name. Something changes within the cells of our bodies, within our inner wounds, within our self-hatred, our guilt, within our longings.

A friend recently shared with me a wonderful poem, written over a thousand years ago by an Eastern Orthodox mystic and theologian. It expresses this awareness with incredible power and beauty:

> We awaken in Christ's body
> as Christ awakens our bodies,
> and my poor hand is Christ, He enters
> my foot, and is infinitely me.
> . . . .
> Do my words seem blasphemous?—Then
> open your heart to Him
>
> and let yourself receive the one
> who is opening to you so deeply
> For if we genuinely love Him,
> we wake up inside Christ's body
>
> where all our body, all over,
> every most hidden part of it,
> is realized in joy as Him,
> and He makes us, utterly, real
>
> and everything that is hurt, everything
> that seemed to us dark, harsh, shameful,
> maimed, ugly, irreparably

damaged, is in Him transformed
and recognized as whole, as lovely,
and radiant in His light
we awaken as the Beloved
in every last part of our body.[1]
   —Symeon the New Theologian (949-1022)

I believe this transformation is meant to include
not only our bodies, our own individual selves and
our communal bodies, but the whole universe as well:
each atom, each molecule, each particle, each world,
each star and galaxy, is to be charged with,
transformed by, changed into the body of Christ.

He will change our weak mortal bodies
and make them like his glorious body,
using that power by which he is able to
   bring all things
under his rule.
   —Philippians 3:20-21, TEV

Surely this does not mean only at the end of all time,
but beginning right now, with every act of love, every
prayer, every shared sacrament.

As these thoughts come to me, I am looking at our
Christmas tree. I delight in Christmas trees and their
wild medley of decorations, those unlikely mixtures of
stars, nuts, kings, clowns, icicles, angels, birds, babies,
harps, gnomes, bells, trumpets, snowflakes, teakettles,
apples, suns, moons, mushrooms, all bonded
gloriously together within the green tree and the
artery-like strings of many colored lights.

What a vision of God's will, God's longing for us all!
We are to suffer, love, feast together in wild contrast. We

[1]From *The Enlightened Heart: An Anthology of Sacred Poetry*,
ed. Stephen Mitchell (Harper & Row, 1989), pp. 38-39.

are not only to love our neighbor but to realize that the more different from us our neighbor is, the better! When we are changed into Christ's "glorious body," it is not a melting down but an *enhancement* of our contrasts, a feast of opposites. We are to dance together in an ecstatic variety as they did on that rooftop in that Greek Easter. We are to shine on one another in the light of our uniqueness as do the ornaments on our Christmas trees.

I think as we grow emotionally and spiritually we enter and share a special sorrow of God's heart. Have you ever prepared a gift, a surprise, a pleasure for another, who did not realize that anything special had been offered? That person was so wrapped up in his or her own agenda and problems that there was no hearing, no response.

A seventeenth-century Christmas carol came to life for me this year. I attended a Christmas service based on this special carol and really listened to it for the first time. As far as I know, *My Dancing Day* is the only Christmas carol meant to be sung by Christ. Christ sings it for us all:

> In a manger laid and wrapped I was,
> > So very poor, this was my chance,
> Betwixt an ox and a silly poor ass,
> > To call my true love to my dance.
> > Sing, o my love,
> > > O my love, my love, my love;
> > This have I done for my true love.

But what if we do not sing? What if we do not dance? There was a ludicrous saying in Victorian times about stubborn, sulky children: "A bird that *can* sing, and *won't* sing, must be *made* to sing!" Fortunately, God is not a Victorian parent! God's power has renounced force. We are given freedom to choose. But there must have been sorrow as well as amusement in Jesus' voice when he quoted an old folk saying:

> We played the flute for you, and you did
> not dance;
> We wailed, and you did not mourn.
> —Matthew 11:17, NRSV

How do we learn to respond? How do we learn to receive God's gift? How do we share the cross and the joy of Jesus' heart?

The realm of love is free. Somebody wonderfully said that the Sermon on the Mount was never meant to be a series of orders and rules, but rather is a description of what we start to do naturally and spontaneously as we grow in the love of the Christ. As we respond to God through Christ, we begin to discover this response is not very different from the way we respond to human beings that we love, longing to give the joy to the other as well as to ourselves.

First, we want to be with God, the Beloved, every moment of the day. We want to share with the Beloved all we feel, all we need, all that grieves us, all that makes us happy, the puzzling things, the fun things, the hard things. This is prayer.

We long to listen to the Other, not just for solutions and answers and advice, but more to learn what the Other is really like. This is equally the essence of prayer.

We learn how to go through the adventure of each day with the Beloved, sharing experiences, doing things together, little things as well as big things, taking the risks of love together.

We want to learn how to love those whom the

Beloved loves, to see them through the eyes of the Beloved. We want to know how to honor and respect them, how to forgive and delight in them.

We begin to honor, love, and forgive ourselves, because the living Jesus not only has compassion on us but *delights* in us. So there must be something delightful in there!

We long to rest and celebrate together, to share beautiful things, to laugh together.

We want to enter into the pain and grief the Beloved feels over the abuse of the body of this earth and those who live in it. We want to be full partners in the healing transformation. We want to share miracles together.

We want to tell other people about the reality of this love, so they can share it too.

We desire to keep our expectancy alert, ready for the surprises of the Beloved, and the still unexplored beauty and power of life together.

We want to delight the Beloved by letting our deep gifts rise with power. For these gifts come to us from the Beloved.

We long to be so deeply rooted and grounded in the Beloved, that we trust the commitment and unity even when we cannot feel anything.

We learn to be active in our response, to *take* as well as receive "Take, eat, this is my Body..." are the words of the Lord's Supper; *not* "sit there passively and be force-fed!"

As we "take and eat," as we enter the feast, lift the cross, join the dance, claim the treasure, we can be very sure that the living Christ receives our responsive hearts with joy immeasurable, radiance unimaginable!

Prayer of Bonding With the Living Christ

Singers and dancers alike say,
"All my springs are in you."
——Psalm 87:7, NRSV

Abide in me as I abide in you.
Just as the branch cannot bear fruit by itself
unless it abides in the vine, neither can you
unless you abide in me.
I am the vine, you are the branches.
——John 15:4-5, NRSV

As you enter deeply in this bodily prayer of bonding with, abiding in the living Christ, know you are free to change any aspect of the prayer and free to stop and dwell on any point. Move through this prayer *very slowly.*

Sit quietly and breathe each breath knowing it is God's own breath of life. Open your palms on your lap, claiming or visualizing the presence of the healing, risen Christ with you.

Place your palms *gently* over your eyes. Be careful not to exert any pressure. When you begin to feel the warmth of your palms flowing into your eyes, inwardly pray: "The living light of Jesus Christ now fills me." Sense, picture, or just think of deep, warm, healing light flowing in and through your eyes, face, and head.

When ready, place your crossed palms *gently* on your throat, without any pressure. When you feel your hands' warmth in your throat area, inwardly pray: "The living *breath* of Jesus Christ now fills me."

Sense, or picture, deep warm light flowing through your throat area.

Next, place your crossed palms over your heart, in the center of your chest. Hold your hands there until you feel the warmth of your hands deep in your chest. Inwardly pray: "The living *love* of Jesus Christ now fills me." Think of, or picture, the warm, radiant love of Christ, filling, calming, healing your heart: perhaps like a warm hand holding your heart as it beats, or a soft light in and around your calm heart. Hold this as long as feels right for you.

When ready, place your crossed hands over your abdomen, at any place that you wish, until you feel the warmth. Inwardly pray: "The living *power* of Jesus Christ now fills me."

Think of, or picture, the deep, empowered love of Christ flowing through your whole body like your circulating blood.

Think now of your feet: "My feet are grounded in this body of this earth that Christ loves."

Picture, or sense, a river of light flowing from the center of the earth into your whole body. Feel or picture it moving slowly through each part of your body, renewing you.

Now open your palms, resting them on your lap, and sense, or picture, the healing light flowing into your palms. Inwardly pray: "My open hands radiate Christ's healing to all whom I meet today."

When you feel ready, flex your hands and gently rub them together. Sit quietly, breathing deeply and slowly. Give thanks to the Beloved, and end your prayer.

About the Author

The Reverend Flora Slosson Wuellner served as an adjunct faculty member at the Pacific School of Religion in Berkeley, California for twelve years. She received her B.D. degree from Chicago Theological Seminary and is an ordained minister in the United Church of Christ. She has been pastor to congregations in Chicago and in Wyoming and Idaho.

She has been an ecumenical retreat leader for over twenty years in the USA and in several European countries, working with groups in the area of spirtiuality and prayer.